Robert Cotton is Rector of Holy T
and is a member of the Archbis
in village churches and a parish
principal of a theological training course. Recently, he helped
to promote HIV & AIDS awareness and other educational work
around Johannesburg. His previous book, *On the Receiving End*
(Mowbray, 1996), explored how to ensure that worship is accessible and nourishing in a wide range of ways. He is married
with two children and a black Labrador.

REIMAGINING DISCIPLESHIP

Loving the local community

Robert Cotton

First published in Great Britain in 2012

Society for Promoting Christian Knowledge
36 Causton Street
London SW1P 4ST
www.spckpublishing.co.uk

British Library Cataloguing-in-Publication Data
A catalogue record for this book is available from the British Library

ISBN 978–0–281–06719–0
eBook ISBN 978–0–281–06720–6

Typeset by Graphicraft Limited, Hong Kong
First printed in Great Britain by Ashford Colour Press
Subsequently digitally reprinted in Great Britain

eBook by Graphicraft Limited, Hong Kong

Produced on paper from sustainable forests

Contents

———◆———

Introduction
Contagious goodness

———•◦•———

'We are a Christian country,' declared the Prime Minister of Great Britain and Northern Ireland, David Cameron. He was not the first to make that statement. When Bede wrote *The Ecclesiastical History of the English People* in the eighth century, England could hardly claim to be 'one country', one people united by customs or religion. Yet Bede wrote his history to persuade his readers that faithfulness to the Christian God, solidarity with our neighbours and personal moral behaviour are woven together. God, Bede claimed, has particularly called this nation to be distinctive in service and behaviour, to be united together and followers of Christ. Since then, bishops, politicians, playwrights, architects and monarchs have rallied followers beneath the banner of being a Christian country, with rhetoric that often falls somewhere between wish and nostalgia. Today the claim is battered by statistics and suspicion. Most surveys can be used to challenge this claim, with barely three million regular worshippers in Christian churches each Sunday out of a population of 60 million. And the claim to be a Christian country is suspect for it sounds exclusive, as though the phrase were a sharpened tool being prepared to damage some (as yet unspecified) group.

Yet many people find themselves somewhere between an intuition that the claim has been historically true and an aspiration that one day it will be more evidently true. How can we, in our day, make these claims more real? One of the necessary tasks is to reimagine Christian discipleship. Most spiritual approaches identify discipleship as involving basic ingredients such as personal belief, Bible reading, attending worship and ethical behaviour. All of these are vital but the missing ingredient is how disciples relate to others. In particular we can imagine discipleship in fresh ways if we concentrate on how disciples do things on behalf of others.

'On behalf of' is an important but dangerous phrase. The Jubilee Sailing Trust is a charity that arranges adventurous sailing expeditions on tall ships for mixed crews, some of whom have physical disabilities. The physical challenge of enabling a sailor who spends much of her time in a wheelchair to take a full part in these expeditions is huge. No less significant is the challenge of how members of the crew relate to each other. The basic rule is: 'Do not offer to do for others what they can do for themselves.' That example reveals just some of the dangers implicit in this phrase. One person can let others off the hook by doing things on their behalf; this behaviour disables, demotivates and infantilizes. Also, the one who is always keen to offer help, to accept extra duties, can end up taking on too much responsibility. These are some of the most obvious dangers as we explore the idea of disciples living their faith on behalf of others.

A positive anecdote about this concept comes from the experience of a senior church leader from this country who attended a conference in the Soviet Union during the 1970s. This was a time of great suspicion, both of western leaders and of western Christians. The bishop knew that his every movement was being watched. Even at the formal dinner at the end of the conference, the bishop knew that his words were being recorded by the microphone hidden in the flower arrangement in the centre of the table. While the first course was being served, as the waitress lent over the table to place a dish in front of the bishop, she whispered, 'My grandmother goes to church.' Her grandmother clearly was of an age that she was no longer vulnerable to losing her job through attending worship. But the waitress was in reality quietly declaring to the bishop her own faith. She could not say so explicitly, nor could she attend worship publicly for the fear of retribution. But the grandmother was actually living her faith in public on behalf of all the family. That is how it is with many people today. Recently a national survey showed that 70 per cent of British people considered themselves to be Christian, yet a considerable number of these neither believe in God nor ever attend church worship. Secular commentators puzzle on this, declaring that the people who reply to the survey in this way are illogical or stupid. But these communities are missing the power of 'on behalf of'.

There are many who, when confronted with the question, 'Do you believe in God?' will feel most comfortable answering, 'No'. They will also deny attending worship. Yet many – according to this poll, 70 per cent – want to be associated with the Christian ethos of this country, a Christian foundation for moral behaviour, churches being a focal point for communities, Christian charities running services for their neighbourhoods, and the vicar being a respected figure who can speak up for the locality. If all this is kept in focus, being a disciple has to be imagined as an exciting, responsible adventure. My discipleship involves me in being the public face of profound things that are going on in other people's lives. Being a public disciple can be the way that allows others to take their first step of faith; it can be that others are saying, 'You lead, I'll follow', or 'You put into words what I but dimly feel'. When disciples are bold in their use of symbols, when they create ceremonies for moments of national celebration, when they worship in a way that makes sense to those unschooled in the Christian dialect, then they are putting on a divine play for which there is an eager audience. The church is a theatre of meaning, and all actors need to keep in mind that the audience matters far more than the actors themselves. The connection between theatre and church, with disciples being public actors for the faith, is a theme that surfaces throughout this book.

So, the first part of this book will explore some of what is involved in living the faith publicly on behalf of others. The title 'vicar' comes from the word 'vicarious', meaning that others are intimately and necessarily caught up in what the vicar does. Some fresh imagination is needed to see that all disciples are to some extent vicars. Being a vicarious disciple can involve you considering, 'Who do I go to church on behalf of? Whose lives and concerns come with me as I attend worship myself?' Though discipleship is a deeply personal matter, actually our church buildings are vicarious places too. So we need to consider how we order our living and our buildings so that others can have the access they need to the God who does not belong to Christians alone.

The second part explores the issues of responsibility that were identified in the example of the Jubilee Sailing Trust. It is easy to shy away from responsibility today, given the fear of being blamed, being taken to court or being criticized in the press for not achieving the highest standards. Yet disciples have also to avoid the trap of taking on too much responsibility. This is partly a matter of their own welfare; moral burnout is common enough. But disciples also want to show their readiness to accept responsibility in ways that encourage others to grow in responsibility themselves. The Christian tradition's emphasis on affirmation, God delighting in us, gratitude, forgiveness and hope combine to form a positive environment in which many virtues can grow. Any disciple will want to consider how to create conditions so that others can flourish too, even if they do not explicitly join in with our enterprise of faith.

The third part looks at the consequences that flow for the church from vicarious discipleship. If we are truly to rejoice in the two-way flow of energy, ideas and possibilities that come from living on behalf of others, the church has to be honest about being a place that listens, hears and responds. We can't do that if we imagine that the truths of God have been completely revealed, and must remain unaffected and unsullied by those who want to hear them. It is helpful to see the Bible itself as well as the Christian tradition as records of listening and exploration. We can then be involved in the sort of listening that changes us so that we see more of God's truth.

It's not easy being a Christian disciple today. The context in which we live is not particularly receptive to some of the values that Christians hold dear. Fragmentation of family, community and national life make it hard to develop lives founded on respect, faithfulness and generosity. Moreover, it appears that there are forces at work in society that explicitly undermine the foundations of Christian living: disrespect for commitment, a perpetual challenge to authority, and protective selfishness. But then these forces make life difficult, say, for those who try to run a charity, a lunch club for the elderly or a Saturday football team. Finding volunteers and maintaining enthusiasm is hard work today. Yet it is hardly an easy time for businesses either. Even though a chief executive has some control over the working lives of those employed, building teams and creating high standards of behaviour (internally and with customers) is still not easy. So I have little time for the lament, sometimes heard today, that Christians and the Church are living in particularly difficult times.

We can, of course, turn this around. Acknowledging that we all face the same sort of challenges in our working, community and leisure lives, we can seek to identify what resources Christians have that can be specially helpful in these trying times. These may be resources from our history, or from our belief, or from the attitudes that mould our behaviour. By focusing on the bright moments (however dark the surrounding sky may be), Christians can not only develop a positive attitude towards being in the Church today but also be models of hope in their other spheres of activity: their working lives, and in their own neighbourhoods. There is a line in the hymn

'For all the saints' which is easy to apply to oneself when the surrounding mood is grim:

> we feebly struggle, they in glory shine.

It's easy to feel that the grass is greener everywhere else. This book explores how Christian discipleship can be distinctive and inclusive, and how we can make particular contributions to building strong communities wherever we are.

Much of this exploration is applicable to individuals as well as to communities. Here I emphasize that the buildings we inhabit, the responsibility we shoulder and the tradition we inherit are best viewed as corporate aids to good and gracious behaviour. I largely use through this book the word 'disciples' to refer to those who are trying to live in accordance with the teaching and beliefs that they uphold. 'Disciples' emphasizes that we are learners and that we are learning from and with each other. 'Disciple' is a more inclusive term that 'Christian' for there are many who want to live the sort of life they know is right, yet for whom the term 'Christian' is an aspiration rather than a current reality.

On 29 July the calendar of the Church of England asks us to commemorate Mary, Martha and Lazarus, companions of Jesus. We know Martha typically as the busy one, to be admired for her practical service (provided it does not become either an expression of self-importance, or a way of avoiding deeper matters). We know Mary as the reflective one, to be admired for her devotion (provided it does not become parasitic on, and dismissive of, those who are practically helpful, or a way of expressing self-importance). What about Lazarus? How do you imagine that the conversation between Jesus and Lazarus went after supper? Lazarus invites Jesus to come up on to the roof in order to enjoy the gentle breeze before dusk and grunts, 'So?' Jesus, recognizing his friend's invitation and allowing himself to carry the baton of the conversation first, describes the hedgerows that he passed today, and the birds he saw. He notes there hasn't been much rain (even Jesus will talk about the weather sometimes), but that they have nearly finished the new bridge across the stream, just outside the village. Peter, Jesus laughs, always the one for the big gesture, nearly fell off the bridge. 'I love him but . . .' (maybe you can work out how Jesus finishes that sentence). Lazarus asks whether they have all got over James and John's rather arrogant comments, knowing that Jesus was troubled by this and had not yet worked out how to deal with it. After a pause, Jesus tries out on his friend a new parable, as he is not quite sure whether he has got the end right. Lazarus, knowing that Jesus likes a bold response, says that the end is right but that the middle section needs work: it's not yet scratching where the very itchy disciples really need it. After a bit more storytelling, Lazarus says he's getting cold, but hesitates to move immediately. For Jesus still finds it hard to confide: and then the words come, 'I'm frightened; I know something big is coming but can't quite see its shape.'

You and Lazarus will know what a privilege it is to be involved in such a conversation which is gentle and spacious, leaving both people in a better place. You will know that, as you compose this scene, you can hear both what you want to say to, and what you want to hear from, God. A Jesus figure who is unable to converse and work out the next step alongside others is as unhelpful as a tutor who knows all the answers. Believing that Jesus had a great imaginative capacity may be as important as our being imaginative with the story of Jesus. Retelling a parable can involve so much more that merely recasting it in modern terms. For the stories no longer belong to Jesus alone; he gave us characters and situations that can fuel and guide our imaginations. As we create, we have to remain aware of the issue of faithfulness: how faithful are we to what was said then and what needs to be said now? This book is partly written to encourage imaginative response in discipleship, when we have confidence to find genuine faithful responses in conversation with others.

7

I remain convinced of the wisdom and grace that can be generated in honest conversations, whether in the staff common room or at the supermarket checkout. Being in tune with one another matters. There is much gracious goodness around. As you go looking for it, you will participate in it. As you find it, you become a carrier of grace for others. Within communities, and between individuals, gracious goodness is contagious.

Part 1

PUBLIC FAITH

1

Sustaining growth

The best Christmas present I received last year was a hedge. I was so excited about this, even when I opened the package to see what looked like 100 twigs stuck in a pile of mud. So I prepared the ground carefully, digging and hoeing, composting and watering. As I did so I had in mind the beautiful song of the vineyard that God plants, recorded in Isaiah 5 and reworked in Matthew 21. God delights in the preparation, in anticipation of further pleasure as the vineyard flourishes, which will be made evident in the production of plentiful harvests. Preparation, growth and harvest are all part of the story – each part bringing delight and joy to the owner. A real hedge takes longer to grow than telling a story about it, so for now I need patience. I can dream about what it will look like in ten years' time, but I also was enormously pleased when the twigs produced their first tiny leaves. Much as I want the hedge to grow I do not want it to take over the garden. An unkempt hedge protrudes over the pavement making it hard for pedestrians, or can smother other plants. I want the hedge to grow in such a way that it will be a backdrop for the flowers in front of it, and so that it will be an attractive border for the property. It will also provide safety and food for the garden birds in the winter. Growth and purpose are inseparable. I want the hedge to grow, but the purpose is located elsewhere – the hedge exists for the sake of the garden.

I find Isaiah's song about the vineyard and my story about the hedge a useful antidote to some of the overblown rhetoric about church growth currently in vogue. The background to this is that I long for the Church corporately, and Christians individually, to be vibrant, courageous and hope-bearers. I do so because I have seen lives transformed by taking seriously the example and teaching of Jesus. More than that, vibrant disciples themselves transform the lives of others, even though these people may not become disciples themselves. Having been in Guildford for fifteen years I am now regularly meeting people working in the town whom I first knew as schoolchildren in our church school. They speak very warmly about teachers who inspired the encouraging creative ethos of the school, and recall with delight some of the school assemblies that I led many years ago. Their lives are clearly different because of these experiences; and they will themselves declare how much they have been influenced for the good. They have 'heard the gospel preached to them' (to use church jargon) but see neither themselves (as hearers) nor me (as the preacher) as failures because they have not explicitly become Christian. If we honestly believe in the active presence of God in people's lives and in the positive influence that these people can have on society, then we must keep confidence in a theology that does not limit salvation to those inside the Church.

So it is possible to be passionate about mission and creative in evangelism, and also not believe that church growth is the prime goal today. Indeed, it could be said that we have yet to hear a sensitive, wise and honest response from those promoting church growth to some basic questions: is a bigger church a better church? Is church growth sustainable? Does God want the Church to grow? Replies to these questions about the institution of the Church will affect all disciples not least because discipleship cannot be merely an individual matter. We are all shaped, encouraged and challenged by fellow believers, and our contribution as disciples to the world is partly recognized and understood at a corporate level.

Consider the first question: is a bigger church a better church? Jesus told many parables drawing on images from farming and ordinary household work. Size often matters; but frequently the emphasis is on the influence of a small ingredient. Matthew 13 records the classic example of a small amount of yeast that leavens the whole dough. Also, there is the parable of the mustard seed, said to be the smallest of all seeds, that grows into a tree which provides nesting space for the birds. The growth is named and affirmed, but the climax of the story lies in the purpose: the provision of safety for the birds. In my experience as a school governor, every few years I find myself asking the head teacher: 'What is the ideal size of this school?' I do so, not primarily to rein in the empire-building fantasies of the head, but to focus the governing body on quality and purpose rather than size. Growing a school can be a beguiling measure of success; by asking, 'Whatever the size of our school, what do you want to achieve?' teachers are reconnected to their vocation of education and development. Equally in church life, we can be beguiled by size, and need to be suspicious of the rhetoric that does not describe any purpose for the church beyond that of being bigger.

The second question is about sustainability. A sustaining church is a church that is a joy to belong to, a church which can be proud of its history, confident in its future, and a church that knows there is more to come from God (though it may not yet be clear what that is). It seems to be countercultural (both in the Church and country) to want to be a sustaining organization rather than a growing one. Many potential leaders seem unable and unwilling to envisage the economy without growth, which is both a sign of lack of imagination and con- tributes to moves towards political and economic disaster. Much the same can be said of some leadership within the churches. Of course, economics is not a zero-sum game in the sense that more economic activity can benefit all without making the rich richer and the poor poorer. Yet it is still worth asking, when the word is used: 'growth *at whose expense*?' There are times that church growth is a cover for, say, 'We want the

Christian voice to be heard more than the Muslim voice', or promoting one denomination at the expense of others. Such sentiments are rarely voiced publicly, but may nevertheless be an important factor in the rhetoric on church growth. There is a further connected question that demands a response: what happens if the local church does not grow? There are plenty of faithful dedicated clergy and lay people within the Church who are not part of a congregation that is growing. The language of growth can be demotivating and disrespectful to these faithful disciples.

Underlying these and other questions are some basic assumptions that gather around the third question: does God want the Church to grow? I have already acknowledged that many of Jesus' parables use the dynamic of growth and harvest. Indeed, the New Testament moves from a gathering of a few frightened disciples after the Resurrection to the crowd of 144,000 named in Revelation 7 (the symbol of a very large number). Wanting the Church today to be part of that move from few to many, it is easy to see that growth can be our hope, our wish, our inspiration: but what evidence is there that it is God's wish too? Psalm 44 is a song of honest recognition that visible success, honour and power are not always in season for God's people. The psalm finishes with the sort of frustration that I hear in church rhetoric today: 'Wake up, God! We sink to the dust – do now what you did in years gone by.' What we don't have is God's response to this psalm. It is commonly accepted that the Church in the West is in a culture where there are all sorts of profound changes happening that make a life of faith hard to sustain – fragmentation (in families, communities and countries), fading respect for authority (in social, religious and moral spheres), withdrawal of trust (personally and corporately) – and the grand religious narrative that gives us a sense of our journey from birth to the grave is less understood and believed. In the face of these and other challenges, why should we suppose that God wants the Church to grow now?

This is not simply a rhetorical question; I would value knowing what signals people have picked up that lead them to suppose that God wishes the Church to grow in our generation. On the other hand, perhaps the Church is being called to be a place where connectedness, honour, respect, learning, trust and valuing our inheritance thrive. Being a church that displays these characteristics in the face of the negative forces that I have already named may well generate a culture that will prepare the way for a resurgent faith. But, as in my story about the hedge, we have to delight in the time of preparation and not merely in the times of growth and harvest. For the Church's message to be credible in a fragmented society we need to use a language about ourselves that is not ultimately based upon one solution for all: that all 'should' become Christian. Such a message will have the tone of empire-building, and will be heard as such by those outside the Church. We need a passion for the Church and its ministry that is founded on others being passionate alongside us, without joining in our life.

Is this settling for second best? I suggest not, and want to describe four particular ways for the Church to be faithful today, each of which has consequences for the individual believer too.

A faithful church today is strong enough to keep going. 'Maintenance' and 'maintaining' have been words of scorn in the Church for a generation; this must change. When out jogging, one of my favourite runs is to leave Guildford behind, go through some ancient woodland and return along the North Downs Way. This is a varied and beautiful route with only one problem: you have to climb St Martha's Hill. Many a time have I run slowly up the first half of the hill only to run out of breath before the summit. By now, I know that the particularly steep section requires me to run for about 50 paces. I start counting at the bottom so that, when I reach pace number 30, I know that all I have to do is run one more step. After pace 31, all I have to do is ensure I complete number 32. Simply keeping going is what is required. One step is enough for me!

At each AGM for this parish, a small part of my annual review is to commend everyone for living faithfully for another year. In a hostile environment that is no small achievement. If 'maintenance' is an uninspiring goal, perhaps we need to talk about being a resilient church. The meaning of this term can be brought into focus by considering what it would be like to be either too resilient or not resilient enough. There is danger in the Church being so rigid, determined or principled that it wins in theory but loses in practice. There is also a danger in the Church being overwhelmed or swept away by the demands that surround us. Whereas in a resilient church, the people will be attentive to each other, tending relationships, encouraging and creating space for celebrations as things go well. A resilient church knows how to set up, develop, maintain and close down. The last of these four verbs is important. A resilient church believes enough in resurrection that it is not fearful of stopping worthwhile activities, for it has enough confidence that God's resources are not fully spent.

A faithful church today looks out for new shoots coming from the roots. I am not a natural gardener, but I do know that some plants – dogwood, for example – will send out new shoots from the roots, if tended and pruned appropriately. We live in an age that is burdened by excessive information, monitoring, quality control and all sorts of bureaucratic processes. Bureaucracy is not the cause of a toxic environment; that, rather, is found in any institution that is unwilling to promote self-reform. Philip Pullman's book, *The Good Man Jesus and the Scoundrel Christ*, is only the most recent attempt in a long line of writing which has alerted us to the distance between Jesus and Christ, the gap between the essence of the gospel and the institution of the Church. St Paul is often seen as a culprit in establishing a self-perpetuating institution rather than proclaiming the original gospel. This is unfair and, within 100 years of Jesus, church leaders were well aware of the need for the Church to be constantly renewing its connection to the original message of Jesus. A self-reforming church will exercise wise discernment to ensure that these signs of fresh growth are faithful to their origins.

A faithful church today values longevity. Many years ago I belonged to a parish where these seemingly apocryphal sentences were uttered in reality: 'But I had to wait 25 years to be asked to read the Bible in church. Why should *they* be included in the reading rota so quickly now?' Valuing longevity is not the same as ensuring that no one can, say, become a churchwarden until they have been in the parish for 60 years. A church that values longevity is a community that knows that some aspects of the spiritual life can only be learnt later. The enthusiasm of new believers is rightly praised and valued. Some wisdom can only be developed after 25 years of faithful prayer and service – knowing how to live with the consequences of earlier choices, pacing oneself spiritually and finding a rhythm of action, recovery and re-action. St Benedict knew this because he required from his monks both stability and a commitment to perpetual conversion. Generations of Christians have found that it takes decades to learn what is involved in each of these, stability and conversion, and also how each supports the other. Once each year in Guildford there is the civic ceremony of mayor-making. A new mayor is formally elected, speeches are given and toasts are drunk. Towards the end of this event, the remembrancer is appointed. This role is now fulfilled by a person who presents a history of the last mayoral year. But the origin of the role of remembrancer was as a debt-collector – not so much as someone who forced repayment, but as the person who remembered what was owed to whom. A faithful church needs remembrancers who, because of their experience of dedicated committed discipleship, know what we owe to God and how we can access grace time and time again.

A faithful church today promotes the health of its neighbourhood. This is the theme to be explored in greater detail through the first part of this book. Using the image of salt in Matthew 5, you know that you do not make a stew out of salt – rather salt draws out the flavours of its surrounding ingredients. 'You are the salt of the earth' is a saying that helps me stand against a well-known phrase, attributed to Peter Drucker, and typical of the brash growth culture I am trying to resist: 'What gets measured gets done.' It's easy to measure how many people attend church, and so the measuring can become attractive in its own right. Measuring influence is far harder. Yet, when the churches working together in Guildford established a Street Angels project, it soon became clear that the streets were safer late at night at weekends, and that the clubbers were being cared for in practical, sensitive and worthwhile ways. The reputation of the Church will have been enhanced in the minds of those who have benefited from this ministry. If this is maintained for another 25 years, church growth may follow. Lurking within all these reflections is a fundamental question: should everyone become a Christian? As I concentrate on being part of a church that is of benefit to its neighbourhood, I am reminded of the classic phrase: 'All may, some should, none must.'

A church that is resilient, reforming and sensitive to God's rhythm inspires responses in those outside its membership. Jesus promised his first disciples that their belief would lead them to do greater works than Jesus did himself (John 14). Similarly, each generation of disciples, in nurturing the faith in followers, can encourage the next generation to do greater works – the followers being younger disciples as well as those outside the faith. That is always a challenge for some Christians: to accept that workers for God's kingdom are not limited to Christian disciples. We are all challenged to recognize that our prayer and other religious obligations cannot be assumed to be duties with intrinsic value. That value needs to be checked against the criterion of: 'Does this action bring benefit to those outside my immediate circle of faithful friends?' The Mothers' Union is a classic example today of an organization that continues to value the fellowship generated within its local groups, and also seeks to ensure that their activities enhance the marriage both of their members and also of people whose families are more fragile and under pressure. Sustaining a faithful presence in the present is a challenge and a worthwhile goal.

So many stories about Jesus are dramatic and dynamic. We are told of lives being changed in an instant. I am often left wondering, 'What happened next?' For example, in Mark 5 we read of the spectacular release and conversion of the man with the unclean spirit, and the consequent drowning of the herd of pigs. The cleansed man was commanded by Jesus to return to his home and tell the story to his friends. So what, I wonder, was he doing 20 years later? He certainly needed resilience and renewal.

In like manner, I treasure the story of the missionaries who eventually reached a nearly inaccessible valley high in the mountains that housed a tribe far from other civilizations. The missionaries were well received and started to tell their stories about Jesus. One night, the tribal chief gave a roar of approval: 'We love the man you are talking about.' The missionaries were delighted. But the chief went on: 'We love this man; he lives further up the valley and he is such a good neighbour.' The missionaries were puzzled until they learnt that, 40 years previously, following a small misdemeanour, a Christian had moved to this valley and set up home. This man had vowed to himself never to talk about his faith, for he had been ashamed of his previous actions. Yet his behaviour over 40 years had been so Christ-like that when the missionaries arrived, the tribe already knew Jesus – for he lived among them.

2

A backdrop of meaning

———•◦•———

Just outside the city walls of Verona you can find the ancient Roman theatre. You have to go through one of the old city gates and cross the river. There, right in front of you, cut into the hillside, you can enter the theatre itself. The audience still sits, as it did in Roman times, on benches cut into the hillside. Some of the original backdrop still stands; some has been restored. This allows performances even now to be heard clearly without amplification. The gradient of the hill is sufficiently steep that those in the top half of the auditorium can, even during a performance, see over the backdrop and into the city. The theatre and the city are tied closely together emotionally, even though, physically, they are separated by walls and the river.

There in the city the ordinariness of life is acted out. Here in the theatre the people are given an opportunity to reflect on, and understand, their actions. Having had the experience we need the meaning. Authors and actors are needed, but they are bringing into sharper focus the sense, order and hope that reside in the experiences of the audience. The beauty, joy and peace that come from being in the theatre are founded on making connections between the otherwise fragmented parts of our lives. Moreover, in Roman times, this theatre was not a place of mere entertainment; that happened in the amphitheatre which is still inside the city. That may be the venue for grand opera today, but 2,000 years ago the amphitheatre in Verona hosted games of death or glory, and the ancient equivalent of

our TV reality shows. Whereas, by stepping for a moment outside the city walls, a different space is found for the sort of
tragedy and comedy that is inspiring and wise. Because this
is the venue for meaning, this is where politics happens –
speeches that tell us who we are or persuade us to be more
than we already are. This is where presentations are made that
challenge, correct or judge our behaviour. The theatre is a place,
not of 'make-believe', but of 'make-real'.

Perhaps, therefore, it is not surprising that about 800 years
later the people of Verona built a small chapel in, and on top
of, some of the Roman theatre. They could have knocked the
disused pagan building down; they could have built the church
nearby (for the stone) but separated (to show distinctiveness).
They didn't. The church of Santi Siro e Libera stands within
the footprint of the theatre, its base being Roman stones, its
walls being medieval brickwork. Over the next few centuries
the church was extended a bit, though its location was never
obscured. Any church is a place of sense, order, hope, beauty,
joy and peace. A few more centuries later at the very top of
the site they built a monastery, a laboratory of meaning. The
people of Verona bring to this site their experiences; prayers
are said; the city is a better place for having this house of prayer
on its border.

You will note that this theatre/church/monastery is 'outside
a city wall'. That phrase reminds us of Golgotha, the place
of crucifixion, being just beyond the walls of Jerusalem. It's
a place also where they stoned the prophets. Being beyond
the protection of the walls makes any of these sites dangerous
places to be. They can be places of rejection, exclusion and
dismissal, for when a city cannot manage either great evil or
great goodness, the people accused need to be ejected. Yet in
Verona, speaking now quite literally, by leaving the city behind,
you have to climb the hill to enter the place which gives you a
new perspective. It's remarkable that the amphitheatre inside
the city, though a much bigger building, is all but invisible from

more than 100 metres away. Whereas the church of Santi Siro e Libera is a marvellous spot from which you can see and be heard. As the bells tolled towards the end of the day to signal the closing of the city gates, the people would have left this spot behind and returned to their town, wiser and more ready to live better.

Many of our churches in England may not have such a magnificent location, but this description can be nonetheless relevant to each community or neighbourhood, and each parish church. Our church buildings are venues of condensed meaning while they remain in a thriving symbiotic relationship with the community around them. Philip Larkin, in his glorious poem, 'Church Going', acknowledges this by describing how church 'happens' when it is properly connected to its surroundings. When this sort of connection becomes truly visible, what can feel like fate is turned into vocation.

I want to explore through this book some of what has to happen for us to be faithful, brave and inspiring disciples. This involves both *me* as an individual being such a person, and *us* as a gathering of disciples. It involves asking ourselves what sort of story we think we are involved in, and what sort of place we reckon our church to be. It involves our heritage and our inheritance, and what we are trying to build on the past that is ours. For, as with the church in Verona, razing the past to the ground to create a flat platform for what we want to do today would amount to losing and destroying rich opportunities. Some of the stories I will tell are clearly symbolic (as well as being true), for we need understandable patterns from the past that help us make sense of our chaotic and disordered present. These stories are not merely analogies, for an analogy is simply a way of dressing up a difficult message. Rather the stories, such as the one just given about the theatre in Verona, are meant to provoke new understandings and insights in you. One role for any disciple is to be a person who is a venue of inspiration, and who finds some connections with others and our past that create and release energy, bringing hope to those whose lives are meandering in greyness. When I first saw the theatre in Verona I felt profoundly moved and saw that the site was a gift to me in my longing to be fully involved with both city and church. But before we become immersed in a story from the 'Dark Ages', I will tell you one more story from theatre-land.

As a schoolboy I was involved in a production of *King Lear*. The rehearsals were not going well; we had learnt our lines and plotted our moves but nothing was coming alive. The whole cast was dismayed. So it was only reluctantly that I agreed to help the stage manager by staying late on several evenings to paint the backdrop. This was an enormous canvas that reached seemingly to the sky; but, in reality, it was stretched from the top of the theatre at the back of the stage, swept down in a curve mid-stage, and reached right to the front. It was the canvas on which we stood, and in front of which we acted. The painting portrayed Lear's kingdom, soon to be divided in three. The whole canvas was a giant map. As we completed this painting, the acting improved. First, I thought this was merely the adrenalin of the approaching first per-formance kicking in. But then I realized that we needed the backdrop for our acting to be recognized for what it was. With no pattern behind us, and nothing on which to stand, we were struggling to make sense.

All disciples need a backdrop. Without this our actions can feel futile and easily misunderstood. Sadly, painting our own backdrop is not that simple as we cannot rely on others knowing and accepting our own patterns of meaning. For example, when I have been out on Christian Aid week, walking a few streets, knocking on doors to ask for money and to present information, I have been faced with such a wide range of responses. Some say, 'I'll give to the Church but I never attend myself' and others say, 'I won't give to the Church because I never attend myself.' I've seen people who want to give money but don't want the literature, saying, 'Please don't tell me about the problems you're dealing with', and others who will take the literature but refuse to part with cash. There are those who feel insulted by being approached for money, and those who feel guilty in not having anything to give. The seemingly simple act of asking for, and giving, a donation is anything but straightforward.

The meanings of even simple acts are dependent on all sorts of factors such as context, intentions, expectations, interaction with others and personal moods. This complexity has been picked up by some theatre directors who, as well as painting backdrops, use gauzes through which we have to watch the actors. A gauze may hide, may interpret the action, or may be removed at a crucial juncture to reveal a deeper meaning. This is something of what it is like to pray with icons. The style of an icon does not include perspective: all is foreground. But as prayer continues, you can be led to see deeper, to see what is within and behind, while your eye never leaves the icon itself.

So as well as benefiting from living our discipleship against a rich and meaning-laden backdrop, we can also see ourselves as acting behind a thin veil of foredrops. The Christian story is something we live towards, and not merely something that happens behind us. Ephesians 4.1 emphasizes this by doubling up the word 'call': we are urged 'to lead a life worthy of the calling to which [you] have been called'. The calling is both something that we have already heard, and also something towards which we move. This sense that the truth is in front of us is articulated also in the prayer which is often used at the end of the *Common Worship* Eucharist: 'Keep us firm in the hope you have set before us.' The Christian hope is a pattern of *shalom* towards which we move; our behaviour makes more sense if it is viewed through that gauze.

Some of the difficulties currently being experienced within the Anglican Communion are similar to those found in any global organization. A complex mix of behaviour and actions is being interpreted against a variety of backgrounds and foregrounds. For example, the Church of England and its leaders, if they speak robustly about the situation in other countries, can be criticized for still inhabiting a colonial world and thereby treating other provinces as though they were still part of the empire of the English Church. At the same time, English leaders can be accused of being weak-willed and lacking prophetic courage if they hold back from speaking out against national or church leaders overseas who exhibit shameful and oppressive lives. The Diocese of Guildford is linked with the provinces in Nigeria. On receiving visiting bishops from that country sometimes we have heard a narrative that makes sense against a backdrop of global antagonistic Muslim–Christian relationships; at other times we are asked for financial support to aid development of schools and hospitals; at other times we are accused of being a puppet of Christians in America. None of these contexts can be denied; living simultaneously within local, national and global arenas is hard. It is not clear that a national perspective should weigh more heavily than local considerations. It must be hard to develop honest, productive and flourishing international relationships between bishops and archbishops who are themselves seen as representatives of their national churches. Nevertheless attention needs to be given to developing close connections between disciples from different nations who are rooted in their local contexts and are daily aware of the potential needs of their communities.

Our humanity and our aspirations of holy living are more evident in face-to-face conversations. Trust grows as we touch each other and walk in each other's shoes. For all his grand designs for peace in his kingdom, Lear goes mad, and only edges towards redemption at the very end of his life as he is held close by the daughter who truly loves him.

The United Nations struggles as much as the Anglican Communion in deciding matters globally and locally at the same time. Moments arise for global leaders when despair seems the easiest option. At times like this I take comfort from the difficulties that particle scientists are tackling as they seek to write a grand unified theory. This theory is meant to combine the interactions of three different types of force within atoms, each of which can be understood on its own, none of which seemingly makes sense of the others. A grand unified theory of church life that makes sense of what it is to be a faithful disciple within the depths of one's own soul, within a congregation, within a national church and an international communion may be beyond the reach of most of us. What I want to describe now is a way of looking at discipleship that gives confidence to live faithfully with fellow Christians, and with neighbours of any faith. This perspective can help us to accept gratefully our particular inheritance and to respond positively to the disorientation and confusion that is prevalent within many modern European countries today; it is sensitive to the benefits and responsibilities of being part of a worldwide Church. This is not a grand unified theory, but is a perspective that deserves attention.

3

Making sense with the neighbours

If you know even a little bit about the earliest period of the English nation you will know two important dates. In AD 597 Pope Gregory sent Augustine with 40 monks to secure the conversion of the people across the sea (now known as the English Channel). Augustine was particularly successful in establishing the foundation which has morphed over the years into Canterbury Cathedral. He used the model of seeking to convert the local kings, their families and their courts, which was successfully taken up over the following 200 years. As each kingdom in England began to accept these new Christian missionaries, so the people started to hear the gospel, see it in action and receive the benefits of a dedicated Christian presence in their midst. We know that there were churches and Christians in the British Isles before Augustine arrived, so 597 was not a radical new beginning. If there was anything helpful to his mission, Augustine used what already existed, not least the social structures that enabled his message to be heard among the powerful as well as the lowly.

The date of the Norman Conquest, AD 1066, is often presented as a time of great discontinuity. England (as it was now known) and the English people had a new monarch and a new ruling elite who brought with them all sorts of new patterns of behaviour. Yet from the point of view of the Church in this land, there was a remarkable continuity. By about AD 1100 the pattern of parish churches serving each town and village (which now seems so typical of the English culture and countryside) was well established. This pattern may have been attacked by the Viking raiders in the ninth and tenth centuries, and adapted by the new Norman rulers in the eleventh century. Nevertheless the close links between local communities and religious houses (to use a term that includes, but is not limited to, churches) had been growing for 500 years and was not broken by military and political disruption. By 1100 the bishops, for example, might be speaking a different language and following different customs (brought in from the Norman provinces) from those which had been familiar only 50 years previously, yet the English church at the centre of its parish survived and thrived. The period from 597 to 1066 is very fruitful for historians, partly because many important aspects of English life find their origins in these centuries, and partly because, with the number of documents and amount of hard evidence being understandably low, interpretations vary. Yet recent research by John Blair in *The Church in Anglo-Saxon Society* and Sarah Foot in *Monastic Life in Anglo-Saxon England, c. 600–900* paint a picture of a developing Church and society that holds great hope for us today in our chaotic disturbed generation.

This period should not be called the 'Dark Ages'. Within only 150 years of Augustine's arrival the Church in England was in a golden age. Missionaries were leaving this country to go to eastern Europe, including lands that had never been completely settled even by the Roman Empire in its heyday. These were not merely one or two inspired individuals (though that is often how the stories are told). This enterprise required a great deal: it needed confidence, a high level of learning about the Christian faith, an understanding of the culture and traditions being encountered, political support and financial backing. At home, Bede may stand out brightly as a scholar of European renown, but he too must be seen as the high point of a widely based network of learning. The Lindisfarne Gospels, to take an example from the field of material arts, did not drop from the skies ready formed, but are an indication of a confident, well-resourced Christian culture – all established within 150 years of Augustine's arrival. One hundred years later England may have been in a parlous state after repeated attacks by the northern people, with King Alfred sometimes said to be the only person left who was fluent in Latin. Yet within the next 100 years, the Church was again flourishing, so much so that reform was in the air, not least because secular rulers wanted increased control over a powerful, influential, confident Church. There was no single cause for this largely successful story, but I want to highlight one aspect that is very relevant for all disciples today.

Religious houses were founded, first by kings, then increasingly by nobles and other significant landholders. To call them monasteries would probably be to mislead; these houses were not built far out in the countryside, in inaccessible places (as happened later, so that the monks could be far away from the distractions of secular life). These houses were not founded behind high walls (as also happened later, marking out a distinction from the surrounding city). These early religious houses were built intentionally close to the local people, a town or village. Indeed they became sufficiently popular that some attracted a population to live around them. These houses might have appeared as some old manors do today, a large enough mix of buildings to support an extended household. There would have been a chapel and feasting room, and accommodation for the religious household as well as guest rooms. Most of these houses readily became successful as they were granted land and farms to be sustainable. The excess produce from the farm enabled charitable work to be practised and hospitality to be offered (certainly to the founding family as well as to travellers). It is very easy to see why a market might also be established nearby. Financial success is attractive, so the town and religious house built each other up. From the earliest days, the monastic tradition (as we later call it) emphasized learning, while also developing the attendant skills of reading, writing and administration. A sufficiently large household allows these higher skills to develop, and so education of the young became part of their vocation too. Once the house was well settled, it naturally became the site for burials and the preservation of the family name, heritage and cultural inheritance.

Such a location presents an attractive picture, being a place that could combine action and contemplation, service and learning, sustainable regular life and also sufficient resources to expand. The heartbeat of the house was regular prayer, though the members of the community probably practised that in different ways. The house may have had a resident priest, but priestly ministry was not essential to the house's flourishing. Some of these houses were founded because of cultural conditions that now seem odd or unfamiliar to modern ears: a royal princess needed, for example, to be removed from courtly life. Royal and noble patronage was important, especially at the beginning, but the pattern was such that, with good links to the local population, these houses would survive long after the founder had disappeared. The religious nature of the common life of the house was vital; it lessened taxes but, more importantly, it provided a distinctiveness that enabled the house to survive in difficult years. Without a recognizable and dedicated religious character, these houses sometimes faded into the background or were actively taken back into the noble family's collection of estates. The distinctiveness that was required for survival came from the style and quality of living shown within the household, and the close links between the house and local community. In later centuries, monasteries concentrated on the former but not the latter. It is this close symbiotic link between religious house and neighbourhood that was so important. As the years rolled on, these houses sometimes became known as monasteries and sometimes as minsters – the two words clearly sharing the same root. By the end of this period, around 1100, some of these minsters would simply be known as parish churches. That is the backdrop (to use the term described in Chapter 2) which can help us understand our vocation today: what we are called to be as disciples and communities of disciples.

A parish church today is a religious house that makes sense of its neighbourhood, and is within its neighbourhood. Members of this household are distinctive in their religious way of life and fully connected to the local economy (in the widest sense of this word). The house will have a sufficient concentration of energy, finance or enthusiasm that the surplus can be distributed nearby. Few houses will be able to undertake all the activities of training the young, extending the faith, nourishing contemplative prayer, practising hospitality, challenging the proud, farming, painting, making music, tending the soil or the sick – but each will develop a rhythm that is sustainable and points towards what makes lives flourish with goodness. Each house will find its way of living 'on behalf of': the prayer is offered *on behalf of* the neighbourhood; and each disciple's act of service is offered *on behalf of* the whole household. Being a disciple requires me to allow others to take pleasure in my attempts at faithful living, and to recognize that I have a contribution to make to theirs. The religious house will be a meeting place for the commitment and talent of all of its members, as well as a place of celebration for the surrounding people.

In our age of easy transport, where we can live in one place, work in another and worship in a third, the intimate link between disciples and their local religious house (parish church) can so easily be undervalued. The experience of the Anglo-Saxon period is quite different, when the town wanted the religious house to help them be what they were. 'We are a better people for having the church in our midst' is an expression that many would like to hear today, and would have been readily voiced (in an appropriately different language) over 1,000 years ago.

In the late Middle Ages, architects, growing in skill and confidence, were able to build spires on parish churches. This architectural symbol is often interpreted as a reminder, pointing us towards God. But if you have walked the byways of England without a map, you will know how useful it can be to recognize where you are as you glimpse a nearby spire. So a spire is also a symbol that is directing our attention downwards: 'The church tells us where we are and who we are.' All this works, symbolically and in reality, without asking the question more often asked in modern times: 'Who belongs to the church?' The close physical connection and ready spiritual links between religious house and centre of population were of crucial significance, and can still be felt today. Some houses had enough residents to offer extensive pastoral care in their neighbourhood; other smaller houses may have been unable to do this, but nevertheless were regarded as places of devotion and dedicated living, which kept a narrative of important times and seasons alive.

This example from history may help us see some of the troubles of today's church in a new light. For example, the endless stream of surveys that indicate church membership and regular attendance are dropping, steadily and continuously, causes much dismay. 'These are the worst of times' is heard, with the expectation that the Church of England and other denominations are only a few years away from complete closure. But the Danes are not raping and pillaging, and the French are not about to invade. If the focus is neither on how many individual Christians attend Sunday worship (the personal level) nor on the international difficulties of being part of a worldwide communion (the international level), we can concentrate on ensuring that religious houses (as I am calling them) continue to be places of devotion, and that they are recognized as such in the neighbourhood. It may take a regular congregation of about 100 people to be able to afford a stipendiary minister; it may take 250 people to produce sufficient spiritual excess that enables a religious house to be seen as a minster (which resources other congregations nearby). But four people meeting together regularly for prayer, encouraging one another in dedicated living, will keep the flame of faith alive in more than just themselves. Problems in today's church often seem to be addressed by considering first ministry and then buildings; I am suggesting we start elsewhere. The task may be to help a small gathering of faithful disciples recognize their responsibility for maintaining a tradition that is over 1,000 years old, of devotion, service and witness. 'Give people responsibility and they will rise to the occasion' might sound too simple, but the history of the Anglo-Saxon period lends its support to this approach.

In the late 660s, England had three bishops. The age of the conversions of the first English kingdoms and the start of the first golden age of the English Church began with a tiny 'hierarchy' compared to today. The role of bishop in Ireland in this period (where there were well over 100 bishops) was very different, with each tribe having an abbot as well as a bishop (the former often being regarded as more senior). The Church in middle and southern Europe also had a different sort of bishop, his role being largely modelled on that of the Roman regional governor. It is this latter pattern that is increasingly regarded as normative and somehow essential to the Church in all contexts. But Anglo-Saxon history disputes that. Bishops were valued for their visitations, moments when the local church could learn from the mistakes and examples elsewhere. But in the absence of the Bishop local initiatives and variety remained, with an emphasis on the quality of living embodied by each religious house – that is what the houses were known for, rather than for belonging to a national church.

This pattern of a high level of local autonomy and responsibility also encouraged the houses to connect with others for mutual support. What we call networking, they developed by forming (to borrow a chapter heading from Sarah Foot's book) 'dependencies, affinities and clusters'. The connections might arise from following a recognized saintly leader or being founded in a particular style. Looking back now we might classify many of the houses as Benedictine, yet intentional close following of Benedict's Rule of Life did not become well established till the very end of this period, in about AD 1000. We are now in a time when some disciples are keen to explore writing their own rule of life. Doing that for a whole congregation, and sharing wisdom from the process and the outcome with other congregations, would be a way of learning from the Anglo-Saxon period.

Though I was just now endorsing the importance of small religious houses, I admit size matters. Part of what is needed is a stable and large-enough community of faith that can welcome, train and challenge newcomers. Induction and formation need to be offered both to the young and to those inexperienced in the faith. Any religious house can be a 'praying unit' and so a visible presence. But it may be only by belonging to a wider network that a full formation in discipleship can happen.

In the final paragraph of his major work *After Virtue*, Alasdair MacIntyre warns against drawing too close parallels with other ages. Nevertheless he describes the start of the 'Dark Ages' as a time when people withdrew from shoring up the empire and started forming new patterns of community where morality and civility might survive. MacIntyre evokes a powerful image of chaos, disorder and reluctance to engage with the formation of public virtues. The story I have told from a small part of English history gives us more hope that faithful disciples can be a positive influence in the whole nation by establishing local places where responsibility, courage and confidence are both embodied and displayed.

4

Finding a way in

————•◆•————

I blame God. Guildford is a lovely place to live, with the river gently running through the centre of town, and the North Downs easily visible from the High Street. Yet there are too many steep hills and, for that, I blame God. Of course, I should blame the twelfth-century Christian community that decided to build Holy Trinity Church just off the High Street. Eight hundred years later, when we were first consulting an architect about building disabled access, he said that he could not have designed a better way of declaring: 'Keep out of my church.' First, the church is withdrawn off the main axis of the street, which means that people still walk along the pavement without noticing it. Second, it is built three metres above the street level, up one of the steep Guildford slopes. Third, there is a fence around the church, with spikes on top, only occasionally pierced by gates. Fourth, even within the churchyard (should you have reached this far), the church is set back a little way. Finally, the door visible from the High Street is not the main door; it is neither convenient to use nor often open, and was hung with the inevitable notice that said, in effect, 'Don't come in here; go around the corner.' Whereas St Benedict in his rule recommended that those eager to join the monastery should not be allowed too easy an entry, the original architects of Holy Trinity took that principle to extreme.

So, for one of our annual Good Friday Walk of Witness services, which finishes outside Holy Trinity, I took as my text: 'Pull this temple down.' Most participants would have heard me allude to Jesus' own words, which themselves refer to his death and resurrection. But, at least in part, I was using the words literally, expressing my frustration, and my aspiration to have 'a temple' less awkwardly placed in relation to its environment.

This chapter is a brief reflection on how people enter, and the significance of what we see on entry. It is applicable to any group that you as a disciple belong to, whether it is a business, a school or a charity, whether it has premises or not, for any group has to mark its territory somehow. If I blindfolded you and walked you up Guildford High Street, you could probably describe to me the types of shops we were passing: the brash music from the high-pressure-sales shop, the fragrance and calm from the perfume shop, and the sudden drop in temperature as you pass the supermarket with its super-efficient air conditioning yet open doors (so environmentally unfriendly). Each declares some values before you even enter the place. Then if we walk in to the building society, quiet on a midweek afternoon, to find the three customer advisers are talking to each other, safe behind a screen, but offering no acknowledgement to us visitors, once again we pick up the values of the organization.

So it was pleasing to hear recently of a new concept: 'virtual police stations'. Since many people now contact the police by phone or by using web-based services, there is far less need to maintain expensive brick police stations, staffed with the officers that we all wish were out in the community. Accessibility can require reliability, so in some local villages, a police officer will be sitting by the village green every Thursday at two o'clock in the afternoon to ensure that face-to-face contact is still offered: a virtual police station. Secular and sacred organizations both have to work on their entry and access requirements. Jonathan, a priest involved with four villages in rural Dorset, operates a similar virtual rectory. His typical Tuesday morning begins with Morning Prayer in one village. Though there is a congregation of only four people, the whole village knows that their church is open at this time, and thereby the rector is accessible each week without fail. After an hour spent in the local school working as a classroom assistant, he cycles to the next village to sit with the police community support officer by the village green who is doing virtual policing. Conversations range from what to do about the rubbish in the ditch just outside the village (indicative that someone is getting out of cannabis production rather quickly) to how to bridge the gap between incomers and aboriginals. The conversation is not exclusive; passers-by stop, listen, contribute and thus participate in the village reflecting on itself. So this is not only the church being accessible (in the person of the rector), but is also about the church enabling the village to be present to itself.

There are times when the movement is the other way: good access provides the church with a way in to the community. Stuart, a minister in the Midlands, takes up his parish's story:

At St Stephen's we too have wrestled – and continue to wrestle – with the question of access, openness and inclusion in the literal sense. A few years ago we decided to establish 'open church', with clear signs on the perimeters by the gates and local advertising in our community magazine. The usual drinks and light refreshments are offered by church-sitters who take their turn on the inevitable rota. We quickly achieved what we had set out to do, and the open church has become something of a local hub for a variety of people, some of whom come for a chat and a cuppa, some for a quiet time, some as tourists on the Victorian church trail.

But more important than the foreseen goals were the unforeseen results. For one thing the church-sitters – quite a large number of people – have all got to know each other far better than before, even if they had been coming to the same church for years. So being open to welcome others has actually built up relationships within the community, and this in turn makes us more welcoming: a 'virtuous circle'. Second, we had often talked about getting a candle stand for the lady chapel but were never sure that the expense would be justified. Once we started welcoming people in, the demand grew and became a real need. No matter how familiar or unfamiliar you are with going to church, no matter to what extent it feels like 'home', lighting a candle is a simple act that anyone can do and feel they have done something. It is a way not only of saying your own prayer but also participating in the ongoing prayer of the wider community. Thanks to a very generous donation we now have a fine candle stand, designed to our specification to fit into the lady chapel, and it is well used by our occasional visitors, our regulars and members of the congregation. Third, open church is regularly used as a venue by the police community support officers as their 'surgery', a good example of community use.

And finally, open church got off to a busy start, but after a while we found that the Thursday afternoon slot was not attracting large numbers of visitors and the sitters were getting bored. So they did some creative thinking about the mission of the church, asked around locally about what might be needed in the community and came up with the idea of a mother/father/carer and toddler group. Now every Thursday afternoon the whole church is turned into an indoor playground, with toy cars, dolls, pushchairs, building blocks and other play equipment strewn all down the aisles, while one corner is a rallying point for otherwise somewhat isolated mums and others who are served tea and biscuits while they swap notes on how to bring up baby and other topics of common interest.

The point is if you really open your doors you do not know who or what might come in. In our case it has been an experience of renewal and refreshment for us as a church, let alone what benefit it might be for those who previously would scarcely have dared to darken our doors.

Back in Guildford, we removed the notice from the door overlooking the High Street. Though it pointed people to the main entrance, the notice actually acted as a visual deterrent. We wanted to keep the doors open, even during worship. But in

February the rain came in, and in July tourists would disturb our prayers to take photos. Doors may be needed, but they don't always have to be shut. Chapter 60 of Isaiah joyfully reflects on what is required to draw people into worship, even if some of these things pull us in different directions. Verse 11 reads: 'Your gates shall always be open; day and night they shall not be shut.' Why have them? If gates are always open, is it not cheaper not to build them in the first place? Yet verse 18 reads: 'Violence shall no more be heard in your land ... you shall call your walls Salvation, and your gates Praise.' Sometimes doors protect us, and sometimes they should be flung open. The mixed messages that come from buildings are not a problem only for churches. Frustrating as it is to be ignored by bank staff who shelter behind their counters, we can respect their need for security screens. For the Midnight Service on Christmas Eve, we shut the church doors so that the drunks do not disturb the worship, and the violence can be outside our borders. So our doors are treasured; some have been repainted, some have been sanded, oiled and polished. For a door can itself be a signal to praise as well as the way in to praise.

We addressed this situation of needing doors to signal a variety of potentially conflicting messages by placing glass doors inside the robust wooden ones. Now the rain can be kept out at the same times as the tourists are looking in. Before the Midnight Service begins, the wooden doors are opened so that the attractions and sound of the church preparing for worship can beckon passers-by. And if we need to, then we close both sets of doors to protect ourselves. Yet you will know that a pure glass door is dangerous since pedestrians can walk into the barrier unaware, literally and metaphorically. I know that in one sacred building, after consultation, those responsible quickly came to the decision to etch on their glass doors, 'This is the house of God': a beautiful, appropriate text. But they could not agree from which side this should be legible. Should it be from the outside, so that those entering know what they are letting themselves into? Or should it be from the inside, as it is a religious text suitable for religious people? Avoiding any words, we commissioned an etching that we hope can be read from either side, a symbol of the Trinity that both reaches down to earth and points to heaven. However much organizations seek to make their literature comprehensible to their customers, the Plain English campaign is needed to hear words as others do. A plain religious language campaign is needed just as much.

So after five years' work, the parish has now removed a notice, polished its front door, and installed beautiful etched glass doors – and the public are still walking by on the High Street, down the steep steps, many feet below. The paths towards our doors are significant and important too. Recent research at Stonehenge has concentrated on setting the famous stones in the context of the surrounding landscape. By now we are familiar with the idea that, at Stonehenge, the inner circle of stones marks out sacred territory; but just as significant are the paths used by the ancient worshippers as they arrived and left. Thirty years ago at one of the then new universities, those responsible for the premises complained at the formal opening that the architects had not planned and completed the paths around the campus. The architects replied: 'We wait for one year, for the students will show us where the paths need to go, by walking the routes themselves. Then we build them.' I wonder how responsive are the groups that you belong to in providing pathways to enter. There is always a danger if those in control believe that they know how what is important ought to be approached. And another danger lies in providing a clear path but hurdles along the way: door buzzers, reception desks and visitors' passes put the visitor in a subservient position, without using any words. The ideal in the Church is that all can approach God on equal terms, as we are all created by God, and all bear God's image. But what about the invisible visitor passes that we can make guests wear? There is a little-known passage in Zechariah 8.20–23 which presents a warm and touching image that combines accessibility, guidance and inclusivity. 'In those days ten people from nations of every language shall take hold of a Jew, grasping his garment and saying, "Let us go with you, for we have heard that God is with you."'

In this chapter I am considering how any group moulds itself in accordance with the values it professes. For the Church, this involves pondering how we are shaped by God's holiness in our personal and corporate lives, in our community and in our buildings. The passage in Zechariah reminds us that the message does not first belong to those who believe, for those outside 'our city' are already seeking the Lord in advance of anything we do. The idea that our buildings should match our character is completely coherent with the image that is much used in the Bible and later hymns, that we are 'living stones, [to] be built into a spiritual house' (1 Peter 2.5), that we are 'God's temple and . . . God's Spirit dwells in [us]' (1 Corinthians 3.16) and in the great hymn of dedication, 'Ye that know the Lord is gracious'.

F. H. Bradley wrote in *Essays in Truth and Reality*: 'I find myself taking more and more as literal fact what I used in my youth to admire and love as poetry.' We do well to look at our church buildings as physical expressions of mission and faith, however awkward they may appear. In a church we worship in the presence of the community of saints from past generations with their embodiment in stone and brick of what was needed to encounter God's holiness. But that holiness takes as many forms as there have been architectural styles down the ages. We have already considered the glorious holiness of God being embodied in our refurbished doors. What of the holiness of God that is engaging, practical and attractive?

There is a church in Sicily that was once a Roman temple. It has been extended many times over the last 2,000 years.

Especially in the nave, where the ordinary people gather, you can still see evidence of the ancient building. In the original temple, there would have been a holy space set aside for the priests to offer sacrifices. For the rest of the building there was a row of columns supporting the roof and marking out the temple space: a row of columns, note, but no walls. Perhaps because the Christians did not like it when the rain was blown in, or perhaps because they wanted to mark out their territory more clearly, by the eighth century the gaps between the columns had been filled in. We now see a wall where there was once a more permeable membrane between sacred and secular.

Many Old Testament stories tell the tale of a frightening, awesome, mystical God; many also tell us of a roll-up-your-sleeves God, a God who makes-do-and-mends, a God who delights in the daily and is not destroyed by our mistakes and misdemeanours. Our buildings, and how we inhabit our churches, need to bear witness to both these truths: that as well as searching for God so that we can be 'redeemed', we also bring to God our ordinary work and occupations. Many of our problems that can be sorted out elsewhere never come to church; but church is rightly a place where we bring those things that do not fit elsewhere. Philip Larkin, in his poem 'Church Going', names both church and earth as 'serious'. What Larkin wrote, John Piper drew in many pictures of churches organically rooted in and growing out of a plentiful haphazard earth. Larkin gives us three words that can characterize church buildings in good use: they are places of meeting, of recognition and of robing. I wonder whether the solidity of our walls makes us better at robing and less good at being places where meeting and recognizing happen.

The frustration that was expressed at the beginning of this chapter, of being responsible for a church positioned halfway up a slope, was not finally put to bed until we had built an attractive ramped access, connecting in an easy smooth way (see

Isaiah 40.4) the High Street and the church. This path connects grandeur and the world; it declares welcome; it proclaims the church as meeting place. And, to use one further boundary word, it makes the threshold less daunting: no steps, no tricky places to stumble. The new ramp is not perfect; we already recognize the need for handrails and better lighting. But there is a type of holiness that is based on intention rather than perfection, on behaviour that is an aspiration if not yet a reality. At the dedication ceremony for the ramp, the con-gregation recited Psalm 24. The questions are asked: 'Who shall ascend the hill of the LORD? And who shall stand in his holy place?' To this the congregation reply: 'Those who have clean hands and pure hearts', not '*We* who have clean hands . . .' The congregation displays its faith partly by witnessing to the aspiration for cleanliness and purity. Later in this book, we will consider the importance of integrity, the matching of words and actions. But for now, perhaps we can recognize the validity of people and buildings acting as a signpost towards holiness.

There is a coda to this story of the developments at Holy Trinity, which is based on the other church in this parish, St Mary's. This is a Saxon church renowned for its beauty, peace and sanctity. Prayers have been said here for nearly 1,000 years. The spiritual presence of the building is evident. This means inevitably that it is expensive to maintain. Peaceful holiness does not come cheap. The west wall, repaired by the Victorians, is in danger of collapse; the roof at the east end is leaking. It is costing many thousands of pounds to fix, an amount of money that could buy a lot of goodness elsewhere in the world. It was a courageous decision to undertake this work, however much we felt that we had little choice. Yet one or two quiet voices whispered: 'Why don't you let the building tumble down and become a ruin?' I don't suppose that these people were antagonistic to St Mary's, its tradition or its people; I am not sure how literal-minded they were being. Perhaps they were declaring their confidence that God's holiness cannot be destroyed by poor or crumbling architecture. There is a large variety of ways in which God displays holiness; each of our buildings can embody and signal some of these. In each building, and whenever believers themselves gather together, we are seeking to be welcoming and set apart, inclusive and distinctive.

5

Orientation

———◦•◦———

Over the last 25 years there has been an enormous change in the way couples prepare for marriage. When I was first a priest in the 1980s, I could watch couples from my study window as they stood on the pavement outside, straightening ties and gathering their confidence, before nervously walking up to the vicarage door. Now, as I flick through a 200-page book on getting married, I notice that a mere two pages are dedicated to the service itself. Elaborate preparations for the reception seem to have replaced nerves with the vicar.

Like some other priests, I have never been fully convinced about running extensive wedding preparation courses, not least because it is so easy for a priest to slip into the role of teacher, judge and permission-giver. Though any one of these roles may be appropriate briefly, the focus should be on making a genuine connection with the couple and allowing their needs to set the agenda. It is the couple's marriage; they know themselves (to a certain extent) and priests can coach them on their emotional and spiritual journey. It is right to ask about families, backgrounds and expectations so that the couple do not merely see themselves as two isolated individuals. It is right to offer insight and wisdom, from personal experience and the Christian tradition, as any couple will benefit from gaining in self-knowledge.

This was the approach I was trained in by the wise and compassionate man who was my first vicar. So at the start of my ministry, I felt comfortable asking gentle searching questions, even though I was a bachelor and well under 30. I would always ask the couple something along the lines of 'What will you do when you have a strong disagreement?' This usually provoked a response that enabled us to have a fruitful discussion. I will never forget the moment when one bride-to-be said, 'That's not a problem, I'll go to my mum's. She only lives on the next street.' I realized that I might not have conveyed well what I was really asking, so I put the question again. 'No, it's no problem,' she said, 'Mum is just around the corner.' I took a breath to ask again, when the penny dropped – the penny dropped for me, not for her. She was expressing very clearly how she saw herself and her role in the marriage: 'I am with my man but, in times of difficulty, I go home to Mum.' She knew her orientation – it was towards her mother, and that was not going to be changed by marriage.

This chapter reflects on the theme of orientation and what is involved in choosing a fundamental direction for life. As in previous chapters, this theme is as applicable to individuals as to communities. Church buildings can help a neighbourhood find and keep its bearings. When a Christian community combines sensitivity and confidence in public faithful living, a whole area can benefit.

The fundamental Christian orientation is expressed in the baptism service with the parents and godparents having to make key decisions. During the recent years of liturgical reform, the range of these responses has grown, and increased in number from three to six, begging the question about how all the responses relate to each other. When I lead people through this long list of questions and answers, I try to give shape to it by the speed and tone of voice. The first three are ground-clearing: rejecting rebellion, renouncing evil, repenting of sin. Without promising to dig out these weeds, nothing of value will really have the space to grow in the heart of the one to be baptized. But ground clearance does not produce a harvest by itself, and so it is actually the second set of three responses that are the primary focus: turning to Christ, submitting to Christ, coming to Christ. Of these three, I feel that the majority of people respond most positively to the first question: 'Do you turn to Christ as Saviour?' Part of turning to Christ is submission and coming, but the central response of the whole set of six appears to be 'I turn to Christ'. This is confirmed by noting that a significant word which is frequently used in many Gospel stories is *metanoia*. This is often translated as 'repentance' but includes every aspect of 'turning around'.

So in a baptism, having clarified what we are turning from, we affirm who we are turning to: Christ. There is a richness in this key image of orientation which is helpful both for those in a moment of transition (baptism) as well as for those who are further on in their discipleship. First, declaring that you are turning to Christ does not imply that you believe every item of the Creed or every verse in the Bible; it does not mean that you sign up for the whole package of Christian truth. Time and again this is the anxiety that I hear expressed in discussion with parents before a baptism: that they think the Church expects them to have accepted and swallowed in full a complete theology that has a response to all known questions. In an age of cautious commitment, I find it helpful to emphasize that they are being asked: 'In times of difficulty, who do you turn to?'

Second, for more mature disciples, although the phrase is 'I turn to Christ', it is good to change the tense occasionally. Throughout my journey with God, I can say. 'I am turning to Christ', 'I will turn to Christ' or 'I am turned to Christ', each of which reveals new aspects of our fundamental orientation. One day, a professor in the Oxford theology faculty was travelling to London by train. He could not be recognized as such, since he was not dressed in a dog collar, wearing an academic gown or carrying a Bible. He was challenged on the train by an enthusiastic student: 'Are you saved?' He replied, 'Am being saved, will be saved, have been saved.' This was not the response the student was wanting but, as well as being the personal experience of this professor, it is an accurate expression of Paul's teaching in the New Testament and an apt description of what it feels like as discipleship develops. Our salvation is past, present and future; but it is our orientation that matters, and that is constant. In baptism we declare who is our focus, our source and our goal. We claim a direction and take a first step.

Helping people to start a journey is as important as being able to show others the way we are already travelling. I have already described how Stonehenge as a place of holiness (for that particular tradition which is now extinct) has to be understood as intimately connected to the paths leading towards it. Recently I have found that this parish spends an increasing amount of time talking about our external signage and notice boards. This is more than a matter of devising attractive publicity. It involves creating signals that those outside can recognize as articulating something that already exists within themselves, and to which they want to respond. We have toyed with the idea of the symbol of putting a trellis on one of the walls of the church so that beauty, a clematis or climbing rose, say, can grow on the outside, yet still be supported by the structure of the Church. What has already proved very successful is a simple poster on our notice board which reads:

BEWARE
Here we practise the inclusive gospel of Jesus Christ.
This means you may be mixing with tax collectors, sinners,
adulterers, hypocrites, Greeks, Jews, women as well as men,
female and male priests, homosexuals, lesbians, the disabled,
dying, thieves and other sinners; white people, black people,
Asians, and people from other races; Muslims, bishops, bigots,
people of other faiths, strangers from Rome and Nigeria, heretics,
etc., etc.; and yes even you, dear guest, are most welcome.
In fact anyone like those who Jesus mixed with is welcome.
So beware, this is not a private club.
WELCOME TO ALL!

Only days after this was first put up, I was accosted by a visitor: 'Can I have a copy?' She did not bother to say what she wanted a copy of, so I was preparing myself to lend her a Bible or a hymn book. Correcting me, she asked – if not demanded – a copy of this particular poster. It so encapsulated her belief, her desire and her hope that she felt nothing more need be said. For years now we have made this available, and sent it by e-mail around the country and overseas. Requests have come also from those who declare themselves to be unbelievers, yet who recognize in those words the sort of God in which they want to believe, and towards which they turn.

Yet however clear the words of a poster or however attractive a sign may be, nothing embodies the characteristics of God better than a person. Whereas any disciple should be prepared to be a signpost to God, being known as a visible representative of God is something we normally expect of our leaders. I hesitate to discuss bishops, individually or as a group, since they are on the receiving end of so many unfair projections and impossible expectations. Nevertheless reflecting on the role of bishops allows us to explore what may actually be required of each and every disciple. So, a bishop is to be an attractive person through whom we can connect with God and find the direction we need to take us forward on our journey. The attractiveness is God's, but the bishop makes this present. In an age when appearance and sparkling charisma seem to matter so much, any leader will find it hard to fulfil this role, especially when leadership at any level includes helping people connect with God and not with himself or herself.

A dangerous phrase that has recently come into prominence is 'the bishop as focus of unity'. The danger actually lies in the concept of unity that is smuggled into the discussion. If you conceive that church unity is about all disciples agreeing on the essentials of belief, then no bishop stands a chance, for many people will be able to find at least one point of disagreement with their bishop; then they have the option to declare that this is an essential matter of belief. Therefore, it can be said, this bishop cannot be a focus of unity. This approach needs to be challenged. The question is not *whether* any one individual can be a focus of unity but *how*. It is a matter of degree or style. In a police force, for example, you would ask of the chief constable *how* she or he is uniting the force, motivating the officers and ensuring everyone concentrates on the right priorities. In the Church by contrast, the danger comes if the starting point is made to be any believer's personal opinion (often dressed up as a matter of conscience). This can make the role of bishop impossible, for any disagreement can be claimed to be so fundamental that unity is unachievable. Anyway, should not the phrase be, 'focus *for* unity'? A church leader is neither an enforcer nor a creator of unity, but has a role within a group of believers of encouraging others to be orientated towards Christ.

When I am bird-watching I am rather an idiot at remembering which way to turn the dial that focuses the binoculars. Suddenly, a bird is pointed out to me that is further away in the trees and I don't readily know whether to turn the dial clockwise or anticlockwise. On my pair of binoculars, in the centre of the focus dial there is another button which can make subtle corrections to the left or right eyepiece, since any person's eyes may not be equally strong. I should not blame my binoculars if I miss seeing a bird. I can't blame bishops if they can see clearly what I can't; but adjustments can be made so that I as a disciple, and we as a collection of disciples, remain focused on Christ. Any group, parish, or organization benefits from reflecting on how unity and a common sense of direction is promoted and presented.

This matter is made more complicated when it is not clear who is inside a group and who is outside. Grace Davie, the eminent sociologist, crafted the memorable phrase, 'believing without belonging' to describe how an increasing number of people associate themselves with the institutional Church. Surveys suggest that the level of belief claimed by people throughout the UK and many European countries remains high although levels of church attendance are declining. Far more people believe in God and regularly pray than actually attend public worship. This is commonly accepted now but there is disagreement about what should be done: should people be taught that you cannot be a proper Christian on your own, and so urged to belong faithfully to their local congregation? The voices carrying such a message can sometimes produce results, but seem to be becoming increasingly hoarse. Or rather, should people be encouraged in their orientation to pray and believe, with the hope that a spiritual life that is developing honestly will gradually want to become more connected with others? Any church leader will know those who could be characterized by the inverse of the phrase: they are those who are 'belonging without believing'. Instinctively these people know they want to be part of a faithful, compassionate, generous group but really hesitate to name their motivating beliefs.

My recent experience in trying to navigate this puzzling area of attachment and disconnection leads me to coin a third phrase: 'belonging without attending'. An increasing number of people see themselves clearly as fully members of this parish, yet they attend worship or other activities only rarely. This was noticeable when I attended a charity concert last year that I knew was a sell-out, yet a quarter of the seats were unused. People had bought tickets, it seems, expressing a commitment to the charity but in the sure knowledge that they would not attend. The expression of commitment remains important; attendance is a different matter. Currently a wide range of community leaders are trying to recognize and understand this pattern of behaviour (which is not limited to church life). Being realistic about the complexity of commitments today, people cry out to be affirmed in the multitude of their obligations to their dispersed family, their work and leisure activities. Yet we can wonder about what is lost if presence is seldom real.

A friend, Mark, took over a parish in Sheffield that had experienced years of difficulty, yet was in good heart. The pivot
of the congregation seemed to be a churchwarden who had
served faithfully for 15 years. Everyone was worried that, on
the arrival of the new vicar, the churchwarden would take
the opportunity to leave. He didn't, until five years later when
he also retired from work. The man took time to visit relatives
in New Zealand, which was a great idea and source of much
joy. Everything was running smoothly so Mark hardly noticed
that the ex-churchwarden had not attended worship for well
over a year. But it became very apparent that something significant had changed when Mark was greeted in the street by
this erstwhile pillar of the community with 'Hello, vicar,
how's *your* church?' Absence had eroded ownership. 'Belonging
without attending' is a potential challenge to any organization
and one that may require subtle adjustment of attitudes and
expectations.

So far the response in this parish has identified three strands.
First, we celebrate festivals as a major time of gathering. Whatever people's intention, whatever levels of belief, it is good to
congregate. We make the most of Christmas, which seems to
come along about once each year. Perhaps the recent rise in
attendance at cathedrals is linked to their ability to be recognized
as places where it is appropriate to celebrate festivals well.
Second, to use a concept promoted by Grace Davie, we encourage
vicarious religion. Those who do attend are asked to identify
who they are attending on behalf of, whose hopes and prayers
they are bringing to worship. Each year this parish makes some
small financial donations to a range of local and national
charities. Once in the year, we invite a representative from each
charity to attend, on a Sunday when our prayers are focused
on their work. As they do so, we ask them imaginatively to
bring their volunteers and fellow workers with them. We ask
them to let their people know that, on this particular day, we
are praying for them, their work and their clients. For example,

the chief executive of the local Age Concern comes faithfully each year, but all of the local branch know that on that day they are somehow vicariously present.

Third, we create special events for they are more attractive than routine attendance. This is familiar territory for many charities as they strive to keep afloat financially each year. A lot of effort can go into running a special fund-raising event, but it is often the regular donations that provide the true financial stability. Routine dedicated support is prized but, when not supplemented by presence, can slowly wither. In parish ministry also the emphasis on events rather than routine seems to be increasing and the consequences can be worrying. It is exhausting running, for example, 25 'special' Sundays each year. For those whose working or family lives are fairly chaotic, and therefore are characterized by disconnected moments, a well-ordered routine may be precisely what the church can offer. Special events don't really create community. As a one-off occasion, the meaning may be solely located in the event itself, rather than the event being an expression of something bigger. People of routine will enjoy a community holding an occasional festival, but they are more deeply connected to the community than a passing expression of fun. Attitudes, behaviour and presence appear to be increasingly disconnected from each other. Patterns of commitment are changing and new ways are needed to ask and respond to the question of a fundamental orientation: do you turn to Christ?

I have already referred to Philip Larkin's poem 'Church Going', which calls our emotional drivers 'compulsions' – an odd description that is worth pondering. We may wish to help others identify and recognize their desires; but compulsions are different from desires. If this generation is one in which what we say we desire is not fully connected to what we choose to do, perhaps the church's ministry should be trying to identify and bring to God our compulsions. A compulsion is not an addiction, but it conveys a flavour of 'something I cannot do without'. To admit to a compulsion is to acknowledge that there is something beyond me which draws, pulls, pushes and beckons me. If I don't respond, I am being less than myself. Church is a place where compulsions meet (for there are a variety of valid and honourable compulsions). Disciples are people who, being honest with themselves, recognize that which compels them and, with prayer, turn destinies into vocations. Finding one's orientation and enabling that experience to be a guide and model for others (whether believers or not) is a serious gift from disciples to this generation.

As we become orientated on Christ, we become people of responsibility and adventure. Those two words provide the central themes of the next parts of this book.

Interlude
Five-dimensional disciples

———————

If you were offered the chance to be more powerful than you are, or more influential than you are, which would you choose? Power seems more highly valued today than influence. For example, something like this is commonly asserted on job application forms: 'In your CV, do not merely list what roles you have filled. Describe what you did, what you achieved and what your particular contributions were to any joint project.' This affirms power; there is little valuing here for being a person of influence. Yet one person being a gracious influence can be such a distinctive presence in a larger group. We should never taste salt in a stew; yet we may barely taste a stew without any salt. For a community to flourish it needs the beneficial influence of salt.

So far we have considered the visible presence of buildings in communities. Attention now turns to disciples. Crucially the focus is not on disciples who plough their own furrow, but on disciples who can enable larger groups to be more fully alive. Many disciples are called to display the sort of goodness that others want to emulate. This is partly about having the grace and humility to be the sort of people who are unashamed and unembarrassed about God's grace active in their lives. Attractive goodness draws people closer to the source of goodness, God. But the movement can be the other way as well: there is the sort of goodness that is confident in being close to others who have not yet been captured by a vision of what is possible. You are likely to feel more comfortable with one dynamic or the other: drawing people close, or coming close to others. Either way, people of influence display a goodness that is not very prescriptive, enabling others to adopt or adapt good behaviour as their circumstances allow. There is a need here for disciples both to walk their talk, and talk their walk.

Lucien Freud, in his portraits, captured some of this as he paints in five dimensions. Freud has a wonderful skill of painting people in 3D: though most of his models are seated or lying down in a small room, their bodies appear real, warm, tangible and mobile. The fourth dimension that Freud paints is the soul, indicating by gesture, tone and colour where the truth of each person is coming from. Yet this is not an absolute science; we can watch people's behaviour and listen to their words, but truth of character is only gradually revealed. At the start of *Macbeth*, Duncan, having been betrayed by his friend, says, 'There's no art to find the mind's construction in the face; he was a gentleman on whom I built an absolute trust.'

The fifth dimension that Freud paints is time. His portraits are sufficiently real, unglamorized and dynamic that you can hear the clock ticking in the background. All this is useful framework for describing what lies at the heart of five-dimensional discipleship; being specific, honest, embodied human beings (3D), who know where their truth comes from (soul), and who can answer, 'What are you becoming?' (time). Freud once said, 'What do I ask of a painting? I ask it to astonish, disturb, seduce, convince.' Those words are equally appropriate for discipleship. Perhaps God says to us, 'What do I ask of disciples? I ask them to astonish, disturb, seduce, convince.'

Such disciples are likely to be influential; quite literally the Spirit will be *flowing in* them. The next part of this book explores this with specific examples that can be useful in themselves or stimulate your own ideas. A recurring question to ponder is: 'How does my behaviour help others to flourish?' Management books may speak about those marvellous moments of being 'in the flow', when your best talents are in perfect harmony with the circumstances and people around you. I intentionally use the image of *flow* too but in a broader sense to indicate God's Spirit flowing in me, and through me to be with others. So perhaps we ought to seek to be people of confluence (as well as influence). This word would affirm the theme that positive attractive behaviour by Christians can make significant contribution to healthy communities. There is an ancient saying: 'One person finds peace; one thousand find salvation.'

So, Part 2 also provides a reflection on how our understanding of moral living can benefit from being based more on corporate behaviour than individual actions. There is an emphasis on general character rather than momentary choices. There is an emphasis on virtues (such as described in the list of the gifts of the Spirit, Galatians 5) rather than rules (such as are given to us in the Ten Commandments). Rules can be used to measure failure; often preferable is an approach that recognizes and values contributions. A central issue in all this is to consider how we are responsible. I am wanting to describe the sort of responsibility that is life-enhancing rather than a burden, that is a joy as well as a duty, and that is freely chosen yet brings benefits to our neighbours. This is part of what is involved in reimagining discipleship which is both a communal and personal adventure, and which can be a positive influence on all who draw close.

Part 2
BEING RESPONSIBLE

6

Taking a tumble

———•◆•———

'Beware of principles,' Lord Peter Wimsey says. 'The first thing a principle does is kill someone.' In normal discourse, we admire people of principle, people who take a firm stand; such people are upheld as shining examples, courageously standing firm in a compromised, morally unclear world. But a person of principle can be the one whose firm stance has the effect of others falling over.

Just before Newlands Corner, the footpath narrows. It's a great route for a run, but you have to be careful here. In winter, it's always muddy and the tree roots can easily catch your feet. In spring, the nettles grow rampant, narrowing the path even more. In summer, as well as all of that, there are brambles. On this particular day, I learnt that there are two ways you have to be careful with brambles. Clearly one is to avoid being scratched as you run past. The other is to avoid treading on one. I didn't. My left foot was planted firmly on one end of a bramble that trailed across the path, which was firmly rooted on the other side of the path. It sounds obvious in retrospect. But in that moment, I just had enough time to realize that I had created the perfect tripping mechanism when my right foot was snared. As I cleaned myself up afterwards and sought to restore my pride, I rose bloodied and wiser. The bramble on its own had not tripped me. What it needed to become a stumbling point was a firm stance on the loose end. Indeed, it is possible inadvertently to trip ourselves up because of our own firm stance. So this chapter is an essay in praise of moral relativism. I begin by asking: why do we want the principles we seek to live by to be more than relative?

One of the supposed beauties of an objective moral principle is that it can be seen as more than a matter of personal choice. If I am trying to persuade my daughter at an early age to tell the truth, I may show her the advantage of truth-telling (a prudential argument). I may then point out that the people she likes always tell the truth (an aspirational approach). Then, at some stage, I will want to convey that telling the truth is simply what we do. I'll say, 'Just do it', a phrase that is trying to take truth-telling out of the range of personal choice, and into the category of objective value. Truth-telling, I am seeking to convey to my young daughter, is no longer related to any advantage that may accrue; it is not a relative principle. In this way, it becomes a reliable habit that is no longer a matter of choice. We know that, when very tired, even our best habits may become less reliable. So it is easy to believe that a basic moral principle should not come within the category of 'personal choice'.

As a priest, I am under the obligation to say Morning Prayer every day. I knew that when I was first ordained; it was part of the package that I accepted. However, in the first months after ordination I realized that I was taking a while to grow comfortably into this habit, and said so to my training vicar. His reply was, '"I don't feel like doing it today" is irrelevant. It is an interesting comment, but we can discuss it after Morning Prayer.' A fundamental principle somehow demands to be followed: regular prayer for a priest; searching after truth, say, for a scientist. The scientific endeavour works because those who undertake it are committed to follow wherever the evidence takes them. In one sense, there is no choice for the scientist; yet anyone experienced in the field knows that how they fulfil this obligation is a deeply personal (and therefore, subjective) matter. Equally, a good human being tells the truth – it is part of the package deal involved in being 'a good human being'.

But how a doctor, for example, breaks a hard truth to a patient, carefully, compassionately, stage by stage, is a matter that is profoundly related to circumstances and contexts.

So I am wary about those who claim to base their behaviour too clearly on supposed objective moral principles. The claim to be merely following one's conscience is made rather readily in some parts of the Church today. It seems noble to say, 'Here I stand, I can do no other.' Whereas I want to ask: what personal choices have you made to reach that position which seems to leave you no other option than damaging someone else? The NEB version of 2 Corinthians 5.14 says, 'The love of Christ leaves us no choice.' That verse expresses succinctly one aspect of the spiritual experience of being claimed by a power beyond oneself. This type of experience may not happen frequently, but it is awesome when it does; and because awesome, other parts of the experience may be less noticed but nonetheless real. So, for example, on one February day many years ago I felt called to the ordained ministry, an experience that, in part, was irresistible. Without denying that at all, I also have come to recognize the myriad of choices I have made (before and after that date) to honour and uphold that experience. Wanting to claim that a moral principle is objective can be motivated by trying to remove it for further consideration. By praising 'moral relativism', I uphold both the awesome character of profound moral principles and the need for the principles to be made real in particular, highly contextual ways, day by day.

The second reason why we want principles to be more than relative is connected with our desire to see them involving us in things that are more than personal. The Ten Commandments were first articulated in a culture radically different from our own, have been honoured through many different ages and are recited today across the world. By signing up to them, I am in part trusting that others are giving their lives to them as well, and are being moulded by them. We belong together partly because we evidently share values. I have always treasured the fifth commandment ('Honour thy father and thy mother') as, at this stage in the Decalogue, the tone of voice changes; there is an earthy realism to this, having heard the first three commandments that refer more immediately to God. So it was with great joy when, on visiting a friend in Hong Kong for the first time, he showed me the Qingming Festival. Families gather on this day to tidy the family memorial, tell stories and share a picnic. This tradition, though originating in Buddhism, is practised by Buddhists and Christians alike. Is that a sign of religious compromise? Or can it be seen as a positive example of moral relativism: a principle of honouring previous generations that is recognized across various religions, and expressed in similar ways? 'Moral relativism' acknowledges that there are similar values expressed in ways that are affected by the surrounding culture, that originate from different histories, and are displayed in traditions that are particular to certain places. The experience is both relative and moral.

Many parishes in the Church of England appreciate music. This appreciation is not limited to that one denomination, but the Church of England has a long and deep history of enjoying music as a way of approaching God. If you come to belong to Holy Trinity and St Mary's, Guildford, you enter into this tradition and are likely to come to appreciate music (even if you did not do so before). It is one of the characteristics that binds our parish together. In doing so, the skill and ability to be moved by music in one person becomes accessible to all those in the parish. I am a better musician having participated in worship here for a number of years. I can't sing any more in tune than before I arrived in Guildford, but my soul has been enlarged by the musicianship of my neighbours. Likewise, I am morally a better person by being close to good people; holiness is contagious. 'Prevenient grace' is a theological term that refers to God's grace which goes before us, or which we discover before any action of our own. To coin a similar term, I have been speaking about 'prevenient virtues', those admirable qualities that we discover already existing in others, that are accessible to ourselves, and that are best described as real (without being objective) and relative (yet more than personal).

Third, lasting values ennoble us by making us ready to sacrifice. Thomas More says to Richard Rich, in the Robert Bolt play, *A Man for All Seasons*: 'Why Richard, it profits a man nothing to give his soul for the whole world . . . but for Wales?' Unless we are consumed by the desire for personal gain as Richard Rich was, we will want to know there are some things of sufficient value that are worthy of our sacrifice, whether of money, time or life. I am not sure of the objective value of the Church of England. Yet I am passionately convinced that God is actively involved in the life of England, and that God's presence can be found in the Church of England. But to go one step further to claim that the Church of England has objective permanent value is 'a big ask'. I love being a priest in the Church of England, and I am in the midst of sacrificing (if that is the right word) my working life for this institution. However, I can envisage the moment, in the wisdom of God, that the Church of England will no longer exist. This thought does not undermine the worthwhileness of the sacrifice now being made by many.

In visiting a cathedral recently, I met a canon who, as he lamented the general poor state of church music, said that cathedrals *had* to keep the English choral tradition going. 'Why?' I thought. Yes, there is enormous value in a tradition that provides great spiritual uplift, marvellously beautiful worship and opportunities for young boys and girls to participate intimately in making such moments happen. Yes, investing time and energy into maintaining this tradition is worthwhile. But to say that the maintenance of choirs to ensure that Choral Evensong is sung from now till the end of time is an objective requirement in cathedrals is perhaps going too far.

Simon Sebag Montefiore has recently published a moving history called *Jerusalem: The biography*. One of the telling features of this book is how often rulers in Jerusalem built monuments and palaces as though they would survive to the last trumpet. Time and again, these buildings were pulled down within the next generation – not destroyed, but reworked and refurbished to suit the needs and whims of the subsequent ruler. Montefiore describes so well the aspiration to finality in a place that has been a perpetual building site for millennia. Success is never final. Many achievements may be worthwhile, but why do we ceaselessly want to make them objective and permanent?

Time and again I hear, but do not understand, people move from 'XYZ is in the Bible' to 'XYZ is for all time'. I am seeking to describe a position that values highly the truths, values and traditions that we read about in the Bible, and yet also recognizes that these are embodied in real living in a multitude of ways. 'Thou shalt not bear false witness' is the seventh commandment, as listed in Exodus 20.7. As a commandment it seems clear-cut until, say, you start considering the annual appraisal that you have to give where describing to a poorly performing colleague all the mistakes they are making may be too much to bear. Appraisals require honesty and no false witness; yet it is matter of discretion to judge how much to say and therefore whether not telling 'the whole truth and nothing but the truth' falls into 'bearing false witness'. The etymology of truth lies with the old English word 'troth' meaning trustworthy. A king is 'true', for example, if his promises are reliable; a judge is 'true' if her judgements can be trusted to be a fair interpretation of the law. The opposite of right is wrong; the opposite of true is unreliable, something that draws you down a wrong path. So if principles, as I am suggesting, are to be classified as true (rather than as objective), we are claiming that they are worthwhile, reasonably lasting, uniting, faithful and trustworthy. That is not a complete list of adjectives. As you consider, for example, 'Thou shalt not commit adultery' you may devise other ways of describing the power and value of this commandment. Such a description motivates action far more than 'It's a commandment; do it'.

So, having pulled myself up after my tumble, I jogged gently up the rest of the hill towards Newlands Corner. Approaching me was a dog-walker who, perhaps understandably, took fright as she saw this panting, bloodied, sweaty mess coming towards her. She moved swiftly over to the left-hand side of the path, as her dog, also taking fright, moved over to the right-hand side, with the extendable lead between them. Had I the breath, I would have laughed, but I did not have enough energy to jump over the barrier they had inadvertently made.

The image I am painting is that of principles and values that are rooted in the heart of God yet are loose at the other end, thereby not being a cause of stumbling for others. The looseness is necessary so that the values can be influential on, and adapted by, others. As I seek to mould my life in accordance with the life and teaching of Jesus, I pray that I am being moulded by the character of God. Something is planted securely deep in my soul so that there can be a harvest of love, joy, peace, patience, kindness, gentleness and self-control (Galatians 5.22). That harvest will, I hope, be encouraging for others; but it has to be realized in such a personal way that others will be inspired, not burdened, helped on their way and not made to stumble.

7

Creating conditions of flourishing

———·•·———

Recently there has been much research into the types of leadership that make groups flourish, written up in glossy management 'How to' books. When such books are published in the
USA, there are usually clear diagrams with four quadrants
as everything, in this field of human endeavour, seems to be
able to be broken down into two axes, four squares, 16 types
and so on. But too much clarity seems to detract from the
experience of flourishing itself, and pre-packages a mechanistic
route towards achieving this that can damage the desire to learn
from our own experience. It is exciting to see the energy and
abundance-making of a group that is flourishing. It is thrilling
to be a member of such a group where the sum is more than
the parts, and yet each part is greater by being associated with
the whole. Better still, it is invigorating to be part of an environment of learning where inspiration is mutual, and we can create
for others profound moments of recognition.

What sort of leadership creates conditions of flourishing?
And what sort of participation from 'followers' creates mutual
flourishing? Can we explore the quality of leadership in an image-
rich experiential way that invites other contributions to finding
answers? Flourishing is best identified in practice. Alasdair
MacIntyre has written a famous book titled *Whose Justice? Which
Rationality?* that displays clearly that what we count as justice,
and what we acknowledge to be reasonable, are fundamentally
matters of choice rather than objective fact. Flourishing, similarly,
is something that we see in action and evokes that well-known

line from *When Harry Met Sally*: 'I want what she's having.' So the approach here is to accept that creating conditions of flourishing is more art than science, and that recognizing it in action is a key part of the task. All participants have to search for the key contributions that make a moment brilliant. After all, most biblical books tell us stories of grace accepted or opportunities spurned; it is only the book of Proverbs that approaches the style of the 'How to' manuals published today, which deserve to be reserved for very wet Sunday afternoons. All this applies as much to disciples as it does to leaders, but I am going to describe it particularly from the perspective of those who have the responsibility of setting the tone for a group. Nevertheless, any disciples can find themselves providing such leadership, whatever their status within a group or organization. So let me suggest some key characteristics.

Seven characteristics of inspiring leaders

1 An inspiring leader can cook

Cooking is important, but not that important. From my experience as someone who teaches preaching, I have found that many books on preaching strive to make you a memorable preacher whose sermons will be recalled long after the congregation has left the church. Why? After all, how many meals can you remember? One joyous thing about a meal is that I leave it behind, and go on my way resourced, encouraged by good company, and heartened by kind conversation. You will see that that sentence did not mention the cook. Leadership often should be similarly invisible; what matters is that people depart from the meal satisfied and strengthened for action.

When I refer to cooking, I really want to include the whole process of meal-making that includes setting the table, devising the menu and washing up afterwards. Finding and arranging the right ingredients is as essential as what actually happens in the oven or on the stove. In a business context, this involves

69

setting the agenda and the process of getting the right people in the room at the right time. But as well as creating these opportunities for nourishment, the cook has to call people together who are hungry and lay before them choices that invite their participation. An old-style cafeteria will slap on your plate a prearranged portion with a 'take it or leave it' attitude. Conversely, a meal can be open-textured and inviting. Such attractiveness is contagious: I am attracted to the food, to the other diners and, by association, I become attractive myself.

Too much purpose can squeeze out this aspect of nourishment. So, in my daily work, I always seek to avoid talking about 'my parish'; it is 'our parish'. Or, even better, it is 'God's parish' because the parish does not belong to the congregation. The parish, literally, is a part of God's earth, a neighbourhood, a living-alongside (the literal translation of the Greek words). We are all guests at the table that is the altar in the parish, and God is the host. The Church can go awry, and dampen spirits, if it fails to act as fellow guest. We may send out invitations, but God is the one inviting.

Soon after I arrived in Guildford, David Howell was standing down after 25 years of faithful and exemplary service as the Conservative Member of Parliament for the town. I did not know him personally, but I recognized immediately that such public service deserved celebrating. We would all benefit from acknowledging and feasting on his example. So invitations were sent out to many from the political, business and charitable life of the town, irrespective of party-political or other allegiances. I was surprised, therefore, to receive anxious phone calls from Conservative Party members. What was I doing? What was my agenda? The assumption was that the church would take this opportunity either to criticize or to further its own cause against David Howell's own party. However, as rector I was trying to fulfil the role of chef and host, creating a feast of celebration.

Similarly, a few years later, the parish was asked to hold an event for a well-respected local charity, Guildford Undetected Tumour Screening (aptly known as GUTS). They asked to book the church hall on a Sunday evening. I suggested that they come to celebrate at Choral Evensong first, and have a party afterwards. They liked the idea but planned to have the speeches in the hall. I countered with the request that the sermon on this occasion would be these speeches, mixed with some reflections from the rector; not that I knew anything about guts, but I did know that GUTS needed celebrating. So another aspect of being a leader/cook is knowing when to say Grace. Does it belong in that transitional moment between kitchen and table, at the start of the meal? Or does an inspiring leader find ways to appreciate and thank from the start of the cooking through to the end of the meal?

For many years, there was a postcard stuck to our fridge with a picture of a family gathered around the table, and the mother standing alongside saying, 'Sorry, no supper tonight; I could not be bothered.' All leaders and cooks hit the wall at times, when suddenly they can lose the will and no longer be bothered to provide. Even then, good cooks do not need to personalize this drama, drawing attention to themselves, but can say (as Jesus did): 'So how many loaves do you have? Make the people sit down.'

2 An inspiring leader is a bit overweight

Julius Caesar said, 'Let me have men about me that are fat.' Cassius was lean and hungry. I imagine that Caesar also was lean and hungry, and so saw Cassius as a threat. Caesar wanted to be unrivalled and so desired fat companions. By contrast, in one international company that is a world leader in its field, the chief executive sends a gift whenever a new senior partner is appointed in one of their subsidiaries: a Russian doll. The message with it reads: 'If we hire people who are bigger than ourselves, we will become a company of giants. If we hire people who are smaller than we are, we will become a company of pygmies.' So if you stumbled into a board meeting, wouldn't it be good to be able to identify some giants (maybe the publicity officer is creatively brilliant; maybe the confidence and skill of the finance officer releases people from worrying about the accounts), and reassuring to recognize some reliable stalwarts sitting alongside the rising stars of the next generation? But where is the leader? Perhaps she is the one who is a bit overweight, not the innermost piece of the Russian doll, nor the master Caesar-figure, but the one who is carrying within herself the future, ready to give birth to talent greater than herself.

You will be familiar, no doubt, with those marvellous and puzzling pictures by M. C. Escher, in which the water seems to flow downhill in a series of channels that eventually returns on itself. By using a trick of perspective, it seems as though Escher has drawn perpetual motion. It may be an impossibility for water to flow in a circle, all parts of which are downhill, but with 'appreciation' it is different. I can appreciate that X is vastly talented (and so I feel humbled and small in X's presence); and X feels the same about Y; and Y about Z; and Z about me. Recognizing and rejoicing in talent is commutative: that is to say, the relationship holds both ways (as, in mathematics, addition and multiplication do). But division is not commutative (four divided by two does not equal two divided by four). Non-commutative leadership is divisive, and increases a sense of hierarchy and superiority, for the boss has to be at the top of the pile. The theological basis for what I am describing lies in the character of God as Creator: the Creator loves the Creation which is itself creative. If we have an image of God as both the origin and the one who rejoices in our talent, then we are likely ourselves to be people who make flourishing happen. Jesus himself followed this pattern, predicting that we would do greater works than he did himself (John 14.12).

We have struggled in our parish for years to recruit volunteers to act as churchwardens. It is a key coordinating role that relies on wardens encouraging, cajoling, leading, cleaning up the mess and generally 'cooking' for the parish. Over the years I know that there were many people who could fulfil this role, yet who presented good excuses for not doing so: having young children, having old children, being employed, being retired, being too busy or being too inexperienced. As I heard the same sort of conversations each year, I began to realize that something else was at work: what I now call the 'Rachel Principle'. For there is in our parish a wonderful person called (name changed) Rachel Jones. Rachel is energetic, spiritual, compassionate, wise, practical, enthusiastic, optimistic and, annoyingly, humble. When people ask not to be churchwarden, one of the unstated reasons can be: 'But I am not Rachel Jones. I can't live up to the standards set by Rachel Jones.' So I have to get my retaliation in first as I approach another person to be next year's church-warden: 'I don't want you to be Rachel Jones, I want you to be churchwarden in your way.' The Rachel Principle is a flip side to the Peter Principle, which states that 'in a hierarchy every employee tends to rise to his level of incompetence'. If Jesus is looking forward to our doing greater works than he did, then perhaps the Church could do with a few more slightly over-weight leaders.

3 An inspiring leader can reheat leftovers

When you don't acknowledge that you are reheating leftovers, it's called plagiarism. Aged 14, I so much wanted to have some-thing published in our school magazine that I found what I thought was a little-known poem and tried to pass it off as my own. I was found out; and the regret and embarrassment of that moment still lives with me. I longed to be part of a tradition of wise insight; the crime was to claim for myself what properly belonged to another. Yet, as I reread these pages, time and again I can vaguely recall when these insights arose, but not fully identify the sources. So I now have a scrap of paper in front of me that reads: 'ABC [my shorthand for Archbishop of Canterbury] – show where serious comes from.' I therefore acknowledge that the prompt for this part will have happened as I listened to Rowan Williams, yet I am neither claiming his words as my own nor suggesting that he would endorse what I write. Leaders must be ready to piece together shards of wisdom, and reheat them to offer nourishment.

Remembering Philip Larkin's use of the word 'serious' we see that one of the Church's tasks is to connect its own words with the seriousness that is found elsewhere. Though there is much talk of vision-setting in leadership manuals, any leader should also be able to tell a history, and to connect the two. The Christian leader is to remind people where we come from, which includes at least these four parts:

1 that we are created by God;
2 that our being remains intrinsically connected to God (that is why we are called 'children of God');
3 that what is so profoundly true about me is also true about you (so, we are inextricably linked to our neighbour and our neighbour's neighbour);
4 that all of this is indestructible.

An inspiring disciple will be able to present that theology in grounded local stories and an inspiring leader will weave such stories together into a larger whole.

As well as looking back, any Christian has a role to help people remember where we are going, our final destination. Since history has many examples of the Church's description of heaven, hell and the final judgement being suitable for one generation and problematic in the next, I have to phrase what I now want to say carefully. If our origin is indestructible, our goal is inescapable. Somehow we are all 'going home'. That does not, theoretically, rule out the existence of hell, nor does it undermine the language of final judgement. God created us and God beckons us back. One consequence of the claim that our return to God is unavoidable is that we are to take seriously what happens in between: 'a serious earth it is'. Good leaders can therefore rustle up a nourishing bubble and squeak, reheating these three familiar ingredients which are leftovers from barely remembered moments: echoes of Eden, intimations of immortality and a seasoning of seriousness.

You may have noticed that this book does not explicitly quote the Bible much. However there is no insight here that is not connected somehow to the inheritance of biblical wisdom. I know that in my prayer and in my living I draw, for example, on 1 Corinthians 1 frequently, as I take comfort and confidence from Paul's creative poetic variations based on God's foolishness and weakness, linked with Christ's power and strength. But I decline to use the pattern that is familiar in some Christian traditions of often pointing explicitly to the source of wisdom, thereby requiring the listeners to find the connections themselves. Each pattern is valid: working from the Bible to experience, and making the journey the other way too. Any Christian can identify a leftover of grace, as it were, God's fingerprint on the world. This person then inspires others to answer the question: what must God be like for us to have experienced grace in this way?

4 An inspiring leader is resilient

There's an enjoyable but simple game to play with young children who have just learnt to count: 'Think of a bigger number'. I'll say, 'Four' and my young daughter replies, 'Five'. I'll say, 'Ninety-nine' and reply, 'A hundred and one' to her 'A hundred'. Soon enough she will say, 'Infinity' to which I respond, 'Infinity plus one'. Whatever number she then makes up, say, 'Infinity times infinity plus infinity and add another infinity', I can say, 'The same plus one'. Then, the penny drops that however far you go, there is always another step to take. This matches a type of proof used by slightly older mathematicians: to prove P is true for all numbers, all you have to do is prove that, if it is true for the number N, it is also true for the number N+1. Actually, you also need to prove P is true for 1; but once, as it were, you have nudged the first domino, provided each domino makes contact with the next one, all the dominoes will fall. Resilient disciples do not have to be able to run a marathon; they merely need to be able to walk the next mile with their fellow travellers. To provide reliable companionship *in* difficulty is to be resilient *through* difficulties.

This also is a helpful way of seeing how God accompanies us on our journey. If we have a mental picture of God achieving anything, bearing any hardship and knowing the result of any travail, we can feel that there is too large a gap between God's experience and our own. This is what I hear in the children's song that begins, 'My God is so big, so strong and so mighty, there's nothing that He cannot do.' Bully for God, I say quietly to myself; that's not what it feels like to me. Yet just look again at the second half of the sentence, which does not proclaim 'God can do everything': rather, it says that there is nothing that God cannot do. This double negative implies something slightly different than merely claiming omnipotence for God. It can be both comforting and reassuring to visualize God as having only sufficient resources to get us out of our current predicament – plus the fact that it does not matter how bad our situation may be. This is what I hear in Romans 8.38–39: Paul names all sorts of threats, antagonistic powers and misfortunes that can come our way, but declares that God can match each one. God's resourcefulness is not so overwhelming that it places us and God in a different league; but it is true that God's resources will not be used up.

I find the picture of a tired yet inexhaustible God matches what I see in the story of Jesus. Brian Wren expresses this beautifully in one of his hymns which speaks of a grizzled, experienced God being wiser than despair. Despair afflicts the best of us, especially when tired. Despair may happen to us; wisdom creates. When I am interviewing a candidate for a new job, I don't want to hear only success stories. I long to hear, when things have gone awry, what wisdom was brought to bear so that new possibilities opened up. That is the resilience expected of an inspiring companion.

5 An inspiring leader has dirty fingernails

Preach boldly, I urge my students, especially with the first sentence. You can win an audience if you map out the territory with the first 12 words. For then the listeners as well as the preacher are already starting to do the work of the sermon themselves, making connections and searching for wisdom. But perhaps I went too far in preaching one Sunday when I began: 'When I look at you I see a rot-pile.' I enjoyed saying that, even if it was a bit naughty.

Now, a rot-pile is the technical term used by foresters to describe a pile of logs, stacked and left behind when the good timber has been taken away. A wood flourishes with a wide range of insects, large and small animals, and places for fungi to grow. By bringing together the wood that has been cut down and not taken away, a sufficient critical mass is created that will promote biodiversity. This requires both gathering and rotting. So my opening gambit was not meant to liken the congregation to a compost heap. It was meant to congratulate them both for being united and for doing the sort of things that happen only when we are sufficiently intimate with one another. In the rot-pile there is warmth, moisture is preserved, a safe haven can be found for mini-bugs and, above all, there is patience and confidence. The rot-pile does not have to look beautiful, be useful or achieve anything. Using this image, I wanted to commend the congregation for faithfulness, humility, perseverance and a readiness to promote other people's growth. Sometimes what is needed in congregations is a positive attitude rather than incessant action. I apologized after the service for my naughtiness.

My scrap of paper also says: 'ABC – beyond usefulness'. In this lecture from the archbishop, the date of which eludes me, I think he must also have been commending the Church to have the patience to let things settle and grow that do not otherwise fall into plans or programmes. Perhaps that is why the Church should be proud to be a place where people come with seemingly intractable problems. A young lad associated with our congregation was criticizing his mother for going to church as, he said, 'It is only a crutch for those who can't manage.' I could not immediately find the way to convey to a 16-year-old that these people had possibly come to understand something that was as yet beyond his experience; that for each of us some parts of our living can't be managed. He went on, 'I don't need church. I have a moral compass; I just choose not to use it.' I applauded his repartee, but believe (mixing the metaphors) that a moral compass is best grown as we live alongside others who are humbly, patiently, faithfully praying. Any rot-pile will be best tended by someone with dirty fingernails.

6 An inspiring leader keeps one seat empty

Elijah has become a slightly mysterious figure in Jewish practice and folklore. In his own day he was regarded as a miracle worker and a robust prophet, one who could speak truth to those in power. Perhaps because we long for that sort of behaviour to be exercised in our own day, traditions have arisen that make space for Elijah in our midst. At the Passover meal a seat will be kept empty for Elijah, a cup filled with wine but reserved only for Elijah, and the door opened so that Elijah can enter. He is the prophet, it is said, who will announce the arrival of the Messiah. This not only influenced the story in the Gospels of Christ's transfiguration, but also makes sense to both Christians and Jews who, in different ways, still look forward to the Messiah's new presence. But Elijah is not just a signpost; according to tradition, he will perform the final miracle before the Messiah arrives. So Elijah's presence will be accompanied by intractable problems being solved and profound disagreements being resolved.

An inspiring leader keeps one seat empty for Elijah. In a straightforward way it is good to maintain sufficient space in a team so that a new member can join without demotivating others. Jesus himself warns about being so fixed in our seating arrangements that hospitality for even one newcomer will literally move someone else down in status. The demotion need not happen if the team leader has established an attitude of spaciousness, so that the team is ready to receive new insight and considers itself not yet complete.

More than that, such a leader will spend time actively scouring the horizon on the lookout for what God may be revealing next. If the leader chooses not to be patrolling the horizon for herself, maybe because of pressing daily commitments, she will want routinely to allocate time to listen to those who are searching for what is on or over the horizon. This is some of what the seat for Elijah represents: making space in the present for what is to come, for that which is as yet unspoken or is coming to the team in a foreign tongue. Of course, wisdom from the past is sometimes 'over the horizon' and spoken in terms that we barely comprehend. A prophet is one who can describe the future as yet unborn, or one who can make present God's truth that has for a while been discarded. A leader can be inspiring by being the one who ensures there is space for the prophet.

The connection between good leadership and positive teamwork is familiar. Yet some teams flourish only because they find their identity in thwarting other teams. Healthy competition is one thing; the inability to co-operate with other teams can mean that a group exists only within a very limited horizon. I am sure that the captain of the *Titanic* ran a tight ship, and managed a good team. But part of good leadership and governance is looking for what is not yet present.

A seat for Elijah is also reserved at every circumcision cere-mony. Elijah holds the door open so that new people can join the community of salvation. In Hebrew, the words for 'stranger' and 'border' share the same root. The one who is beyond our border is likely to be a stranger and, if a stranger, then possibly a threat. But Elijah is the reminding symbol that the one who is beyond may be the source of our salvation. So the inspiring leader will keep alive for the team the truth that health and salvation is as much a matter of import as it is of export. For example, a well-run dedicated team of responsible 'service providers' will want to bring health and well-being to their community – and also be ready to recognize and appreciate how the community brings health to them. One empty seat is a powerful symbol.

7 Fill in the blank here

There is more to inspiring leadership than has been named so far. But the list will be a better one with your contributions. A complete list invites criticism; I would rather invite your participation.

For my part, I will briefly describe a bishop I knew, working in South Africa, who embodied much of this chapter. Bishop David prayed and his people knew he prayed. David cared and they knew he cared. He was familiar with the contours of souls, and he was comfortable contributing to international symposia. David was an absolver for he knew the pain that flows from sin, and the freedom that is possible after sin. David worked tirelessly with, and supported, those caring for families affected by HIV; he had defended his people in the last brutal years of apartheid but, in more peaceful times, he would have been a mystic. He might have been the tallest tree in the forest, but others grew around him; his shadow was protection, not a curtain on growth.

The picture of Bishop David is not complete without mention of 'journey', for he was always future-orientated. The acceptance

David offered was real, yet as conversation with him warmed up it merged seamlessly into finding a new and better future. David knew that leadership can involve taking people where they do not want to go, but his big-heartedness ensured that people were largely willing to be taken on such a journey.

These elements are encapsulated in a grace-filled moment that begins with a breakfast. Sharron, a priest in his diocese, had been invited to visit a parish in Washington, USA, which supported their work in South Africa. Sharron was to be accompanied by two teenage girls from the townships who had, until then, never travelled more than a few miles from their home. To put them at their ease, a few weeks before the trip, David invited the girls with Sharron to breakfast near the airport so that they could become familiar with what the journey would involve.

David listened, encouraged and gave assurance. He told the girls he was proud of them. As the meal ended he suddenly realized that they had no luggage. So he strode off, determined to find just the right suitcases. Sharron and the girls could hardly keep up with his great paces, but instinctively knew that it was safe to follow wherever he was going. Not satisfied until he had found just the right suitcase for each girl in the right colour, the right size, the right style – David was profoundly equipping them for the journey. As the girls, a few weeks later, flew into the unknown, they were carrying with them – or, indeed, were being carried by – a bit of that grace-filled man.

David was a person of potential; he saw it in others, he knew it for himself; everyone felt more potential in his presence. When he died, his friends mourned but knew they were living better lives because of his company. David was big in spirit, but self-effacing. We benefit from being familiar with, and carrying within ourselves, our own personal examples that connect us with the presence of God's Spirit.

I was reminded of Bishop David as I read recently this review of a concert: 'The conductor was simply concerned with getting the best out of his players; he inhabits both score and orchestra, offering a seamless conduit between the two.' The conductor made not a sound, yet the concert hall was an enchanted place that night because of his presence. Not all disciples are called to chair committees, run groups or manage large organizations. But any true disciple will be able to offer some of the spiritual leadership discussed in this chapter, which is a leadership evidenced by creating conditions of flourishing. Equally, any disciple will want to identify and work alongside such inspiring leaders.

8

Living with mistakes

————•◆•————

'I dwell in possibility,' writes Emily Dickinson. In her short poem of that title, she paints an attractive and evocative picture of what it is to dream. In the house of possibility there are so many windows on to the world; the only limit is the sky; the chief occupation is 'gathering paradise'. Possibility, she declares, is 'a fairer house than praise'. I doubt that Dickinson would react favourably to my changing her quotation thus: I dwell in responsibility.

Responsibility is the name of the house found in the parable of the talents (Matthew 25). The master of the house bestows on the servants talents, time and opportunities. What we know, because we know the end of the parable, is that the servants will be held responsible. In fact, in being made responsible, the master is declaring that their actions are worthwhile, what they do matters. Thereby the servants are deemed worthy of trust. Moreover, as the servants will be held responsible they are drawn into relationship: they are acknowledged as partners with the master who has given something to them, takes an interest in them and will want to hear from them. To be given talents (and, by association, using the modern word, to be acknowledged as talented) is to be recognized as important, worthwhile, active, and creators of meaning ourselves. Responsibility is a fair house where residents have the chance to create paradise.

Yet, responsibility can also be a sombre place. It is common to hear about 'compassion fatigue'. Too many responsibilities are placed before us, exacerbated by an increased awareness of disasters overseas and neediness at home. The very people who are best at offering immediate generous kindness are those who, because of their highly developed sense of responsibility, are starting to feel burnt out. This fatigue has only increased recently as it appears that a growing number in our communities seem to have found a way of being inoculated against responsibility. They read the same papers, listen to the same disaster appeals and walk the same streets, but do not see what needs to be done, nor what they personally can do. For others, 'you always have the poor with you' (Matthew 26.11) is such a demotivating sentence, which leads them to want to take a compassion holiday. But the experience of muting the cry of the poor can become a habit. Also, in a blame generation, taking responsibility is dangerous, as anything less than perfection so readily generates criticism. It's easy to say that we once knew how to live with situations that went awry. Mistakes happened through negligence, weakness or deliberate fault, and it was only the last of these that truly caused difficulties. So I find a proportion of volunteers are happy to make particular contributions to charitable activities, but will not take general responsibility, and so are not prepared to give an account of the whole story from beginning to end. Responsibility is a house with vacancies.

Never trust a consultant who cannot describe what they have done wrong and how they have lived with that. When conducting interviews for people who want to be paid to offer my parish or charity advice on matters to do with finance, or buildings, or personnel, say, I will hear stories of how the consultant has turned situations around, leveraged in new capital, or enhanced tired buildings. Success shows competence. 'And what,' I ask, 'when things go wrong?' It's not an unfair question – or, at least only as unfair as asking any candidate in interview, 'What are your weaknesses?' Generally, the potential consultant will be able to describe what went wrong, quickly to be followed by what they did to put it right again. Whereas I am pleased to hear how that person can recognize failings, not run away from difficulties and take initiatives, I am actually listening out for how the person can live with mistakes. The role of the macho-consultant is always to provide success and turn around failure (which is only ever temporary). Such a person is hard to trust as the moment my situation seems unresponsive to action plans, the consultant will head for the door.

In this part, I am wanting to delight in responsibility and reclaim it as an attractive place to dwell. But responsibility cannot be a key and attractive aspect of discipleship if we cannot face and live with those moments when the concept does not seem relevant. How can we let our responsibility go into 'idle mode'? To use an analogy, a mad-keen football supporter must be able to deal with situations (such as the death of a relative) without always referring to football. Without that ability, enthusiasm turns into the sort of fanaticism that can be very damaging. Equally, we can rejoice in humans being 'the animals that are responsible' and yet recognize that situations occur where the concept is not appropriate.

Holy Trinity Church, Guildford is a beautiful church for worship; and the parish is fortunate to have a spacious church hall. But these two buildings are not connected and that causes difficulties. We have found files containing proposals from 40 years ago to extend the church so that there would be a meeting place which is an integral part of the church building. These proposals were taken no further than a small committee; but ten years later they were reactivated, and ten years again after that. Finally the parish managed to bring forward plans that could be submitted to English Heritage and the local planning authority. I could tell a story about this which would include the familiar ingredients of vision-setting, consultation processes and fund-raising. But, for now, the story will pick up from the moment when we, to the surprise of many, failed to secure planning permission. All the elements had seemed to be in the right place but they said, 'No'. Hopes were dashed; aspirations thwarted; many felt bruised, battered and exhausted. A terrible part of this was that, in the final four weeks, the congregation fractured into various groups and the parish leadership was unable to find mutually acceptable common ground. The archdeacon called in a consultant to start the healing process. But this person could recognize only that everyone had seemingly behaved well, all the right processes had been followed but – with a shrug of his shoulders – it went wrong.

Now what? There was nothing much we could do. The rejection from the planning authority was so strong that there was little likelihood of appeal or changing minds. And it truly felt that there was nothing much *to be done*. Yet, every Sunday we had to face each other in worship – babies had still to be baptized, sermons preached. There is not much room for the blame game within a group of people who want to stay together. Some wanted to blame me and I wanted to blame others; but that would have been a false path back towards activity. Fractured arms need to be set in plaster, not amputated. The broken arm is no good for action, until healing is complete. Responsibility was not being denied, it was just being quiescent. One of the toughest conversations to be had was with a person who had publicly voiced an opinion different from that held by the parish leadership. He had to be asked to step back from his role as a chalice minister, someone who distributes the consecrated wine at communion. Some would not have been able to receive the sacrament from him at this time of hurt and anger. Space needed to be created but he was not being excommunicated. He needed not to receive this as punishment. For we belonged together even in the midst of the pain that we had caused for each other.

Trust was required on all sides: trust in each other, and trust that, with faithful prayer and continuing service, God would heal. An overdeveloped sense of responsibility would have propelled any one of us into asking, 'What can I *do* now?' It would be a short step from that to the continuation of the struggle. So perhaps while responsibility sleeps, trust continues. Who is it that said, 'History is written by the victors'? Many claim these as words from Winston Churchill, and so they seem to find a place within a context of belligerent struggle. I would rather say that responsible victors can ensure that the stories of all parties are told, for then responsibility builds communities and holds a variety of voices together. The last stanza of the Emily Dickinson poem I quoted earlier begins 'Of Visitors – the fairest'. The house of responsibility also welcomes many guests who, in bringing a variety of opinions, need to bring trust and patience as well.

So, that was an example of a situation when it was good to refrain from action, and therefore not to enquire further about who is now responsible for what. There are other situations when the central feeling is rather one of pointlessness and uselessness. Responsibility is hardly worth mentioning at such times for it simply seems an irrelevant concept. Ironically, it is while on retreat that I have often experienced the 'uselessness of prayer'. For at least one month in advance, I eagerly look forward to my annual retreat. I spend days dreaming about the walks I will take, the books I will read and the music I will listen to. In the last few days before my retreat, I will then realize that I have already overfilled the days so that, if I were actually to attempt what I had in mind, I would need a week's holiday after the retreat. So I jettison these good ideas which have largely arisen because I want to make good use of my time. In trying to be spiritually responsible, I have squeezed out peace and certainly left no time for listening to God. So, with my original plans left behind, I arrive at the retreat house ready for prayer. It is a joy to enter a familiar chapel, light a candle and settle down into centred stillness. Because the mind takes longer to settle than the body, I find myself thinking about people I have left behind. I try to turn these thoughts into prayer. It's good to pray for people in a leisurely way.

As the first day passes, I am becoming more settled, having abandoned my diary and current commitments to God. I find a new stage begins when, having remembered others, it is easier now to pray for myself. Being used to this process, I know this is not selfish; after all, I am on retreat partly to offer my reflections of the last year, and my hopes for the future, to God. But as the hours pass, it is becoming harder. Many years ago, I seem to remember 'hearing God's voice' but I wonder how that actually happened, or whether it is just a convenient way of speaking about God. Others certainly seem to hear God's voice more frequently and clearly than I do. Now, silence descends. Prayer feels harder; and that is usually one step away from feeling that prayer is pointless. 'What earthly use is this?' I feel useless; and then I experience 'the uselessness of prayer'. I am not saying or hearing or doing anything; any action seems pointless; my sense of responsibility no longer functions.

This territory will be familiar to many other disciples. We do pray and we want to pray. But knowing what is happening, and describing what we are doing when we pray is very hard. So let me go back over what has just been described and explore with you three aspects of prayer. These will be familiar to you, whether you are used to making a retreat or not. First, we pray for people in need. When your aunt is sick, you will readily visit her in hospital if you can. You will send flowers; you will pray. It's a quite natural thing to do even if we express ourselves in a language that has not changed much from our childhood: 'God, please make auntie better.' Time and again I meet people who are so pleased to know that they are being prayed for by me or by the church. These are not necessarily believers themselves. Disciples pray and should be unashamed about that. Do it; name it and others will thank you for praying. You may not know what response you get from God (directly), but those who know you are praying will be grateful.

Second, beyond praying for situations lies praying for people. On retreat, I will eventually forget what my churchwarden is worried about – but I will remember I need to pray for her in herself. The outcome matters less – we do not need to tell God either what we want or what God should do; the person, who is the centre of our prayer, matters more. Intercession turns into remembrance, and remembrance into thanksgiving. If you have ever held a distressed baby in your arms in the middle of the night, you will have experienced this. Fifteen minutes of 'praying for' leads into a simpler naming the child before God: 'Remember young Jimmy – he is precious – I am so glad he is here.' Appreciation is a close cousin to thanksgiving. As we spend time being grateful, we come to appreciate more of the complexity and connectedness of life – we appreciate how much we are given, and how we are connected to the One who gives. In Hopkins' poem, 'As Kingfishers Catch Fire' there is the beautiful phrase: '[he] acts in God's eyes what in God's eyes he is – Christ.' This phase of prayer, which is so often beyond words, takes us into a time of seeing 'what in God's eyes' we truly are.

Third, disciples confess. For some, this is the easiest way to begin prayer: to unload the burdens and mistakes of the day, to name the fractured situations that you have been aware of, and to acknowledge your involvement in the hurt that flows from this. Confession can include naming those moments when things have gone awry, and not merely when specific faults have been committed. One of the early desert fathers said to a young monk who was worried that he had nothing to bring to confession: 'Confess the sins of the world, if you have no sins yourself.' Confession involves so much more than mere personal mistakes.

Though this sort of prayer can feel rather dismal, it is worth giving it time for it can be a door into something much more profound. Slow confession can make you aware of a long dull ache in the soul. If you have patience and courage to attend to this, you start to be aware that you are being given to realize how a small part of the world is not what it could be. Perhaps you start to glimpse the shape of how things could be different. This prayer is similar to the sort of conversation you can have only with a trusted friend which begins by not even knowing what you want to talk about. If you know what the problem is, you could probably hazard a guess at the answer. But you need to trust your friend not to scoff or interrupt; you also need confidence that the friend's energy may be your lifeline and guide as you enter into the darkness. When I am ready for this phase of praying during my retreat, I will pray sitting in front of an icon. I need to close my eyes to withdraw into prayer. But I also need to be able to open my eyes occasionally, to be reassured by the icon of God's presence, and to reconnect with the truth that the icon depicts. This sort of prayer begins in dissatisfaction, yet actually expresses a profound longing. Most mature disciples will accept that both are a normal part of faithful living. Even though the content of this prayer is largely beyond words, and so this prayer is difficult to do and to talk about, any Christian community is strengthened by publicly making this a part of their common life. It was only through the encouragement of others that our parish established a monthly time of silent prayer, intentionally offered in a public space in one of our churches. Many have been sufficiently grateful for this dedicated time that I reckon that people have been praying like this for years in private, waiting for more public recognition.

The connecting theme of this part is responsibility. This is an unavoidable aspect of discipleship. But this claim cannot be made if we can't also fully integrate into our discipleship those moments when responsibility is an unhelpful concept. Discipleship does not stop when we are fatigued, when we make mistakes and don't know what to do next, or when we are fractured or when we are taken to a place beyond helpful action and usefulness. Discipleship does not stop, nor does responsibility. But both may take a rest. So, as I drive away from the retreat house, I leave rested and refreshed, ready to take up my responsibilities once again. And, more than that – I am reconnected with those aspects of life that are beyond my control and my influence. I find God through my being responsible: I also know God's presence in those times that are beyond. For a community to flourish, as well as having people of responsibility, it needs Sabbath people: those whose lives embody ease, centred-ness, and an ability not to be distracted. Sabbath people make Sabbath time happen. In the midst of busyness they are not scared by inactivity; in the midst of responsibility they are not frightened by acknowledging that there are things beyond their control. We all benefit from being with people who know that you cannot pass from Saturday to Monday without going through Sunday.

9

Willpower is not enough

————•◦•————

This part of the book has been exploring whether we can say that responsibility is a necessary component of Christian discipleship. The chapters have been seeking to understand the characteristics of responsible discipleship, especially in the ordinary throng and press of life. But to see whether responsibility can be seen to be an unavoidable part of our living, Chapter 8 looked at some of those moments when the concept seems irrelevant, unusable or impotent. The suggestion was that disciples still can, and need to, see themselves as responsible beings. Yet we can still acknowledge that there are times when responsibility sleeps. There is one other area of human experience that needs to be considered: does responsibility end with death? If, to put it even more strongly, responsibility fades towards death, does this actually tie the concept only to those active moments in life when we are energetic, busy and creative? If this were to be the case, then disciples would have an excuse or an opportunity to switch off from being responsible some time in the twilight years. So the question is: are we always responsible as disciples?

I should have known something was wrong when I heard laughter on the other side of my bedroom door. I was lying quietly in bed, excited and anticipating all that might be about to happen on my tenth birthday. But it sounded as though my family were enjoying themselves without me, outside my bedroom. Then they opened the door and walked in together, holding something small. It is said that the smallest presents are the best, but this seemed very small indeed. In fact, it was only a card. Clearly they had been enjoying the message on the card so much that it provoked outright laughter. I was given the card; the picture was of a person looking wistfully into the sunset and the message read, 'Who will look after the world when I am gone?'

This was a painful moment of self-understanding. My parents and brothers knew me in a way that I, being a ten-year-old, did not yet know myself. The implication of the card seemed to be that not only was I used to getting my own way and organizing whatever I was involved in, but also that I did not really trust anyone else to do it as competently or as fully as I would myself. After all, who would look after the world when I was gone? I managed to laugh with my family – for even I could see that a bumptious ten-year-old might benefit from being brought down a peg or two – but I felt the message sink home.

The virtue of responsibility is flanked by two vices: being irresponsible, and being too responsible. This chapter will reflect on the latter. This is not merely a matter for one individual, as an overdeveloped sense of responsibility can demotivate others. Chapter 7 explored something of how responsible discipleship can grow and flourish within groups. By looking a bit more at the vice of being too responsible, we are actually trying to identify some particular qualities of 'good responsibility'.

Disciples should leave room for chance. Harold Macmillan might have called these 'events, dear boy'; we should be on the lookout for how we can contribute positively within 'events' that happen to us. For example, Guildford Diocese used to run a cricket team for which there were two strict entry requirements: that you knew which end of a cricket bat to hold, and that you could run 22 yards without needing your inhaler. Now they run a highly talented team, but in the years when I played, we were required to have only those two skills. Still, we had fun, and opposing teams enjoyed playing us for obvious reasons. To encourage us, one day the wife of a team member brought along a bottle of champagne which she declared that she would give to the person who produced the champagne moment of that match. Two hours later, I was standing near the boundary when the batsman launched the ball majestically towards the clouds roughly in my direction. I knew that this was hopeless before I began, but I had to give chase. Up and up the ball went, as I ran around the boundary towards the spot where I expected to pull the ball out of the nettles. Still it went up, still I ran, till I began to realize that the ball was going to drop somewhere near me. I suppose all of this lasted only a few seconds but it felt far longer. I stuck out my hands so that, at the end of a 50-yard dash, I caught the ball. To others it seemed effortless and a matter of perfect judgement. To me, I had merely run as fast as I could and held out my hands. There was no contest at the end of the match as this clearly was the champagne moment – except, as she handed across the bottle, I dropped it.

The catch was a fluke, unrepeatable and enjoyable. Of course, I intended to catch the ball in the sense that I wanted to and hoped to catch it. But I did not intend (in the sense of planning and setting out in my run at precisely the right speed to inter-sect with the ball) to make the catch. Being a good member of the cricket team only requires intention in the former, wider sense of the word. That is to say, cricketers must remain alert and want to do well all of the time, but they are not required to draw up a plan and execute it for every over of the day. The same is true for responsible disciples. Being alert and having a will focused on God is required and can be practised by any disciple, whatever age and whether in the midst of life or close to death. The purpose here is to recognize how we can be responsible in situations other than those when we have a plan, execute specific actions and evaluate a goal (that is, having an intention in the strong sense of the word).

Another example happened in church, not on the cricket field. The rector stopped in the middle of the Old Testament reading during Evensong. Concern rippled around the congregation. We thought he might be ill or possibly have something stuck in his throat. But he looked up and, with a pitiful look on his face, said, 'I simply can't go on.' What I can't remember is what he was reading; I know for sure it was a chapter of either Proverbs or Ecclesiastes. Whichever one it was, I suddenly understood something new about the nature of the Bible and our response to it. Let's suppose he was reading Proverbs. There are many good verses in Proverbs which, taken on their own, guide us into understanding human behaviour and how we should live. But try reading 20 or 30 verses in a row. What is instructive in one verse becomes didactic after ten verses, and sounds like an instruction manual after 20. All vibrancy is excluded and the Spirit is deadened. That's what the rector experienced and he had the courage to say that he could not go on. One proverb may be wise; lots of proverbs squeeze out chance, inspiration, or the grace-filled moment. The book of Proverbs needs Job, which is a book that begins in tragedy and ends in God's presence. Even Job's comforters are worth listening to for their warped theology provokes Job (and us) into an extended search for a better truth and a deeper connection with God. On the other hand, the rector might have been reading Ecclesiastes, which was probably written by someone who had drunk too much Proverbs. The author drones on: 'There is nothing new under the sun.' No one should read Ecclesiastes without the Song of Solomon close to hand. Whatever Old Testament book the rector was reading, he experienced that too much of one sort of behaviour was damaging. Even with the Bible some books need a partner. Proverbs is needed as a response to the histories (where there can be too much chaotic charismatic yet disordered behaviour). The Psalms may be quite varied, but Psalm 119 benefits from being balanced by the joyous freedom of Psalm 150. Proverbs and Ecclesiastes give us a responsibility that is so dutiful, so well intentioned (in the strong sense), so well thought out, that chance does not happen. As has been said, disciples need to leave room for chance. We do well to beware of overdosing on responsibility, however unavoidable it may be.

Before leaving the champagne moment, I want to highlight one further aspect. Being part of a good situation, even though you may not be able to identify precisely your contribution, is a way of being responsible. The cricket captain has to decide where to place the fielders and who will bowl. The captain is clearly responsible for those particular choices, yet the team members have a role to play and should not switch off. Discipleship includes being part of a moral team, often at different levels. Corporate morality is exercised on a grand scale, for example, in the fair trade movement, at a community level within a congregation or small business, and also within small networks of family or friends. All this is in addition to making personal moral choices. The kingdom of God, in Jesus' teaching, is both dependent on God's action, and also requires our participation and contribution. As well as both these elements, the kingdom of God 'happens'. Part of being a disciple is being ready for these happenings. Stanislavsky, the great Russian theatre director, said, 'Leave a revolver on stage. Someone at some time will use it.' That saying is a marvellous affirmation of trusting actors to be ready for unplanned moments. The revolver is not required by the stage directions, but may one day be precisely what an actor needs – probably not to harm, but to create the sort of effect that opens up new possibilities. In like manner, God provides, and unplanned moments of grace happen.

So far I have wanted to loosen the connection between being responsible and the strong sense of intention. We can still act responsibly in the midst of contingent circumstances and as part of a team when we are not directly instrumental in making the key decisions. There is one further aspect to this that I want to name.

Responsibility requires effort but is not solely dependent on effort. Or, putting it another way, we are called to act responsibly throughout our lives yet the range of responsible actions changes. For example, a young person may need to make a wise decision whether to experiment with drugs or not; at some stage later, the same person can decide whether to back off and change their behaviour. Further on, the choice may have narrowed down to complete abstinence or death. Recently a notorious drug-user was reported to have lost her battle because 'she was too tired to fight her demons'. Each day of her life she was responsible, even until her end, yet the range of choice was gradually narrowed.

I did not find such an understanding of the changing quality of our willpower as I read *The Good Book: A secular bible* by A. C. Grayling. This is presented as a book of wisdom that is not reliant on theology or the history of God's teaching as delivered by Moses or Jesus. A very brief précis of Grayling's message could be 'Try your best', but the emphasis is on 'the best' with no mechanism for dealing with situations when effort wanes and energy is lacking. 'Give of your best' is different. That is what I hear in the story of the feeding of the five thousand. Jesus creates the situation where the young boy can offer whatever he has. That offering is sufficient for enabling the miracle to begin. Effort is needed but, with God involved, effort does not completely determine the outcome.

Finally, we can approach an answer to the question that was posed at the start of this chapter: does responsibility fade towards death? It has already been shown that we are called to be, and can be, responsible throughout our lives, even when we are not in control of ourselves or events. Billy Connolly, as he enters his fourth decade of being a superb entertainer, is reported to have said, 'My ambition is to be very good at what I do, keep standards very high, and stay dangerous.' These words brilliantly combine effort, energy and an affirmation of quality, with a desire to be appropriately 'on the edge'. I can picture Connolly entering his hundredth year – maybe no longer able to hold an audience of a thousand in hysterics – but still dangerous: keeping the staff in a nursing home on their toes, and laughing at their jokes. Our morality and our spirituality must be held together. We are not released from our duties in this life until the very end, but our focus can be on the One who is calling us home. The last verse of the hymn 'Forth in thy name, O Lord, I go' is:

> For thee delightfully employ
> whate'er thy bounteous grace hath given,
> and run my course with even joy,
> and closely walk with thee to heaven.

We are still called to make best use of all our abilities, even as we walk the final steps with God to heaven.

Many of these reflections were originally stimulated by a parishioner called Shirley, on the day after her mother died. The final few weeks had not been easy as her mother had been distressed, spiritually not physically. I was expressing sympathy but Shirley understood what had happened. 'My mother had a hard time at the end of her life. She was always moralistic in her religion, which left her nothing much to draw on at the end.' Powerful words! A religion solely based on morality tends to become moralistic. The book of Proverbs on its own eventually becomes tedious, dispiriting and judgemental. Morality is not squeezed out by spirituality at our end. At the margins of our existence, good behaviour, a good understanding and a heart orientated towards God belong together.

Part 3

COURAGEOUS
EXPLORATION

10

A memoir of explorations

————•◦•————

Thus far we have recognized the importance and necessity of a two-way flow of energy and ideas between disciples and the community in which the disciples live. Discipleship exercised on behalf of others means both that we are open to the agenda and concerns of those outside our Christian tradition, and also that we are responsive to what we hear. Anyone who has been on the receiving end of a purist counsellor who listens and listens yet never speaks will know how unnerving this can be. Although, when in difficulty, we want to be heard, if the person listening to us is not affected by what is said then we will feel that we are not being taken seriously. So the question of integrity needs to be addressed. For it could be damaging for everyone if we sought to live as vicarious disciples within a church that was itself unyielding in doctrine and practice. Equally, people are put off if our communities paint a picture of a granite-like, unbending, eternally fixed Bible. There's little merit in developing a strong personal rapport with those outside the faith if our message is based on an inflexible church preaching from an unresponsive Bible that teaches about an unyielding God. This chapter looks at one aspect of this: reimagining discipleship requires us to reimagine the Bible.

You could consider: how large, do you imagine, is the full stop at the end of Revelation 22? This is the last chapter in the Bible. Does the final full stop say to you, 'End, finish, nothing can ever be added to this'? Historically, the process of settling the list of books in the Bible took about 150 years, ending in the fourth century; even then, different traditions ended up with slightly different lists. But, before that began, nearly all traditions had come to agree that there was a distinction between God's word that came to them in the ancient writings, and God's continuing direction that was revealed in prayer and discussion day by day. There were fierce battles with heretics who wanted to blur completely this distinction. But all orthodox traditions came to agree that there was metaphorically a big full stop at the end of the Bible.

However, the belief that the Bible could not be changed does not imply that the meaning of what is in the Bible was fixed for ever. What is recorded in the Bible is exploration, even if the extent of the Bible is settled. The solidity of the final full stop should not mislead us as we seek to understand the amazing fluidity of changing perceptions of God. New contexts emerged in the 2,000-year period that is the historical backdrop to the Bible, and people of faith came to understand more about the mystery of God in changing circumstances. That is what will be investigated now: that the Bible is complete and dynamic, reliable and revealing; and that, in a similar fashion, disciples are to be faithful and adaptable.

Just outside my study window, I can see a flock of more than 20 rooks circling a copse. It seems that they are looking for a safe place to land. It's remarkable how they seem to co-ordinate their flying and their decision-making. But then, in a moment, the pattern is completely disturbed. Perhaps a sudden gust of wind, or the glimpse of a predator, has startled them. Now, it's hard to discern any pattern, as they seem to be shrieking at one another and nearly colliding at times. A group of three separate from the flock and approach one tree, ready to land – but the others don't follow, and the squabbling resumes. Smaller groups fly off in different directions, testing this landing place or that; but co-ordination seems to have been replaced by competition. Just as suddenly, a decision is made and the flock settles, all together on different branches of the same tree. The unity of the flock is very attractive: 20 flying together, 20 settling together. But what happens between these two moments is vital: the noisy disturbing chaotic arguing is what leads to finding the safe landing space.

I want to start by examining the nature of the Old Testament. We both misread the Old Testament, and also do not use it well as the ally it can be, if we regard it as a rather low-quality bread-and-butter pudding: a way of using up old, stale and stodgy experiences, occasionally enlivened by a juicy saying. How about instead viewing the Old Testament as a memoir of explorations, a mix of voices calling us to a variety of attitudes, behaviours, hopes and visions? If we listen carefully to, say, Exodus, we will be drawn in one direction: journeying, leaving behind, confident that God is with us. But that will be a beguiling or dangerous voice to hear if our context is harsh, traumatic, or in need of radical overhaul: then we will better draw sustenance from Jonah or Job. The rooks may have a favourite tree in the copse, but if a raptor is lurking there today, they need to settle elsewhere. The opposite of 'right' is not always 'wrong'; the traditions recorded in the Old Testament supplement, nuance and balance each other. Each deserves a careful listening to and proper attention.

For example, on a normal day when my life is the usual mix of compromise, good intentions and moments of ill-will, I treasure the all-too-human stories of Abraham, Sarah and Isaac. These are real characters who, with the benefit of hindsight and the glow of looking back from a safe distance, are admirable and honourable forebears; yet these people are also at times dishonest and cowardly. This tradition is very realistic and earthy, from the start of Genesis 2 onwards: we are created out of mud and blood. Passions are real and deep: 'Adam' wants 'Eve'; Cain murders Abel. From these moments forward, God's character is just as passionate: all but destroying the world in the flood; knocking down the builders of Babel; God's mind changes and God gets angry. God is presented as the tribal leader, Yahweh, who calls forth equally passionate leaders who honour this particular name for God. Because this is all so anthropomorphic, the stories are easy to tell and remember.

I could not live under such a God for long without needing some peace and respite. So there is another tradition that describes God in far more lofty terms. This is a mystical, transcendent God who bears the name Elohim, Lord of hosts. For this God is the supreme being in a well-stocked heaven; and we humans are addressed by God's own messengers. Jacob, for example, wrestles with a stranger at night (Genesis 32) – this cannot be God's own self, but is a being authorized by, and representing God. As anyone knows who has struggled profoundly in and with the darkness of their soul, God remains the same but we can become a new person; Jacob leaves the story with a new name, Israel. This tradition gives us Moses and the burning bush, an equally life-changing mystical moment; this is not the law-receiving Moses of the Ten Commandments, but the prayerful Moses who can enter the cloud at the top of Mount Sinai to become one of God's messengers himself. This tradition is ruthless in its attacks on kings and priests who enjoy the privilege of being God's close companions but do not live up to that calling. In historical terms, these two traditions become increasingly entwined, but their original distinctive qualities (of how we see ourselves and God) are valuable. Yet neither tradition (on its own, or combined with the other) was what the people of Israel needed in the seventh century BC.

From around 650 BC onwards, for a few generations, the Kingdom of Judah based in Jerusalem had relative peace. Troublesome neighbours had been absorbed into other empires; cultic centres based at Bethel and in Samaria had been destroyed. The journeying and tussling of the older traditions already described were not relevant or responsive to the settled prosperous times now. So a new understanding was articulated that focused the people, priests and monarchs on keeping the law (Torah). That was the way to honour God, who nearly disappears from the account apart from the role of being the moral God, dispensing law. The people of Israel feel they own their kingdom not because Yahweh lives in Mount Zion, but because they are the people who have established and keep God's law. Looking back, this third tradition gives us as models for our behaviour many great stories about upright successful kings, and wicked unsuccessful kings. Ironically, David is the chief exemplar whose alleged faithfulness and moral behaviour are not always ideal. Even bad behaviour points us towards the uprightness of God (which is what is required of us too). This tradition is given voice in the charming anecdote of a troubled Jew who visits his rabbi and says, with great worry: 'I no longer believe God exists.' The rabbi replies, 'It doesn't matter whether you believe God exists; just do what God says.' Yet the increasingly apparent absence of God as a personal force can make this tradition strident, harsh and judgemental. It becomes violent against outsiders (and is probably responsible for some of those stories recounted in Judges and Joshua about the slaughter of the indigenous people in the 'Promised Land' which disturb us so much today). The tradition often speaks with a rhetoric that implies that we are on the brink of a golden age. 'If only' is a key phrase; if only we behave properly, if only we put in a bit more effort . . . This tradition is well represented in church life today.

The golden age did not happen. The Babylonian Empire conquered the Kingdom of Judah and all the movers and shakers were deported to Babylon. Oddly, the group of people which had lost most in the exile were the ones who wrote afresh the fourth great tradition found within the Old Testament. The priests had lost the temple, and so had lost their business, their role and their purpose. Yet it is the priests who summoned up an understanding that God is permanently present, in the best of times and in the worst of times. They retold the story of the exodus not as a release of slaves who would conquer and enter into their own land (as the previous tradition did). For the priests, the exodus was a tale of God's continuing presence in the desert; God 'tented' as a nomad with the people. The book of Exodus finishes with an elaborate and ornate description of the tabernacle, for that is where God is, and God's glory fills the tent. This exodus story finishes on the brink of the Promised Land, for Israel is not a people who dwell in a particular country (according to this tradition), but Israel is a people who live in the presence of God. Some stories from this fourth tradition were dropped into the narratives written much earlier, all of which are characterized by God's continuing presence with the vagrants: Adam and Eve leaving Eden; the murderer Cain protected in his wilderness journey; Abraham leaving his first homeland to find his final dwelling place. John's Gospel uses one of the key words in this tradition in the well-known verse: 'And the Word became flesh and pitched his tent among us' (John 1.14, trans. Nicholas King). This word affirms that we don't only need an all-conquering God, we don't need only a God who is supreme and beyond, we don't follow merely the tribal leader God – what Jesus embodies is God who is faithfully with us.

So God is passionate, transcendent, moral and present. In response, disciples are called to be committed, mystical, upright and faithful. Those who are familiar with biblical scholarship will recognize that what I have presented is a very brief summary of how many of the historical books of the Old Testament were composed. The four traditions recognized by biblical scholars match four distinct ways that disciples are called to pray and live today.

Holding together such variety is not easy, either in church or in community life. In 1999 I was part of a group responsible for allocating grants to community groups within our borough, which wanted to mark the millennium. We devised a set of criteria that was meant to help us evaluate the various applications for funds. The first time we used the criteria we found that they were too general, allowing all but the most hopeless applications to be 'above the line'. So we tightened the criteria but, in discussion, found we were accusing each other of prejudice: 'You are only making that a criterion so that your favoured bid can secure funds.' In the end, the outcome appeared satisfactory; grants were awarded to a firework party for Millennium Eve (a thing of the moment), the planting of an avenue of trees (long-term and orientated towards the future), a sculpture (intentionally placed in the centre of a village, proudly local) and a stained-glass window (evocative and pointing to 'beyond').

In a similar way, the biblical traditions nuance, correct and supplement each other; none should seek to override or dismiss another. As it is said, 'Only the whole church can hold the whole truth.' One consequence that flows from this is that we should value our history and the changes that arose because contexts for faithful living radically altered. To see the Old Testament as fixed and somehow etched in stone is to miss its vibrancy and to close down its role of provoking us into new patterns of faith now. The count in Giuseppe di Lampedusa's novel, *The Leopard*, says, 'If we want things to stay as they are, things will have to change.' Or to put it slightly differently: if you do the same thing when all around you is changing, you are not doing the same thing.

So far, I have described the four spiritual traditions that created the stories recorded in the history books of the Old Testament. The other chief element of the Old Testament is the prophetic books. The three major prophets are each rooted in these traditions, and show how each tradition copes with change: Isaiah is based on the passionate/mystical God; Jeremiah on the moral God; Ezekiel on the present God. Each of these books was composed over an extended period of time probably by a 'school' of prophets, though I will call each school by one of these three names. The adaptability to changing circumstance of each tradition is further important evidence to support the claim that the Old Testament does not merely give us static norms for our behaviour, but requires us to ask: if they lived and adapted like that then, what are we called to do now?

The book of Isaiah was composed over the longest period. Around 700 BC, Isaiah was based in the northern Kingdom of Israel and steadily lost faith in the rightness of the king. The human 'tribal leader' was not matching in behaviour what the divine leader required. So Isaiah's prophecies always contain judgement and promise: 'We know the *shalom* that God will bring, but not while we have this sort of king on the throne.' The northern Kingdom of Israel was absorbed into the Assyrian Empire in 701 BC and a similar threat faced the southern Kingdom of Judah in around 590 BC. Exile happened, which should have been the end of the story for this tradition. After all, what is a tribe without a land? What use is a God without a people? But the key innovation given us by Isaiah came in the darkest hour: that the God of Israel is the only God; and so Yahweh is the God of all and not merely the God of Israel. The vision that Yahweh God has an intimate connection with all people is one that the Church, in its more tribal moments, continues to find hard to uphold. But there was one more massive change that the tradition of Isaiah had to cope with, that of the return from exile. How easy it would have been (and still is) to revert to a tribal God when restored to one's own territory! But in the final chapters of Isaiah the prophet seeks to find words of comfort that hold his people to the under-standing of a universal God, who is still dedicated to the welfare of this people, and who requires our shabby behaviour to be changed to match God's righteousness. I like to keep this history in mind as I work within a church that at times wishes it had its own territory to rule, at other times despairs that it is in exile among aliens, and sometimes forgets how to be distinctive.

I reckon that of all the three major prophets the miserable prophet Jeremiah dealt least well with change. In the first half of his book Jeremiah goes on and on indicting Jerusalem for disobedience to the Torah, declaring that the city will be punished and proclaiming that the enemy assault is the will of God. Jeremiah sticks with his vision of a people called to be in a covenant relationship with God. Even in the wonderful prophecy (Jeremiah 31.31) of a new covenant which promises that the law will be written in the hearts of the people, it is still a covenant limited to the house of Israel and Judah. Jeremiah does not reach the same universal understanding of God's role as Isaiah. Yet in the middle of his book, Jeremiah finds release from the pain of losing his land and acknowledges that it is worth living faithfully even as aliens: 'Seek the welfare of the city where I have sent you into exile, and pray to the LORD on its behalf, for in its welfare you will find your welfare' (Jeremiah 29.7). As well as faithfulness to the law, Jeremiah is telling his people that they need confidence (not confidence in the rightness of their cause, but confidence in the character of God), courage (not courage for the battle, but an enduring courage to face the long haul) and a wisdom that, though rooted in knowing the past, generates fresh insights for now. There are plenty of Christian writers today who are vocal in their denunciation of our secular age and describe powerfully the fading of the Church's authority. But these authors rarely seem to acknowledge that we will reach the promise of the new covenant (Jeremiah 31) only by first passing through the time of 'seeking the welfare of the city' we are currently in (Jeremiah 29). We may be resident aliens but we need to put down roots where we live now. Holding back from seeking the welfare of our neighbours now, Jeremiah says to his people, is irresponsible behaviour.

Ezekiel knew the pain of being present among an 'unclean people'. Ezekiel worshipped a holy God, which was perhaps easier for the tribes wandering in the desert than for the exiled population forced to live in a foreign land. The desert purifies us towards holiness; a foreign city can easily be felt to be a dirty place. Yet for all his longing for the distinctiveness that comes with being set apart as holy, Ezekiel stands in the tradition that gives us one of the most famous inclusive phrases: 'You shall love your neighbour as yourself.' This is not merely the neighbour who shares your jokes, your values and your history; this is your foreign neighbour. Moreover, if you feel dirty living in this foreign land, hear both parts of the sentence: love your neighbour, love yourself. Indeed the complete verse (Leviticus 19.18) bars you from vengeance or bearing a grudge – behaviour that is easy to adopt when feeling bad about yourself; and the root of this loving is given as 'I am the LORD'; the holy God is present with us. The key innovation that Ezekiel's priestly tradition adopted was that all the people of God were to live according to the purity laws that had once been reserved only for the temple personnel. There are no second-class disciples. If there is no longer a real temple served by real priests, then collectively we are all to be the temple, and all to behave as priests by praying on behalf of everyone to God, and accepting a representative responsibility.

This chapter has been an attempt to paint a picture of the Old Testament that shows it as an intriguing, exciting resource for disciples who are prepared to face honestly the tribulations of today. As we listen to this collection of books, we hear a conversation between different traditions, each confident of their own vision and teaching, yet each better for being not the only voice in the room. What is more, each tradition has had to face how it has needed to change in the light of traumatic events, especially precipitated by living for a while in exile. My experience of conversations within church structures is that it is hard enough to get traditions talking to one another, and it is even harder to hear how traditions acknowledge their own developments.

Yet we can make the same sort of mistake in our personal life of faith, by being too rooted in one tradition at the expense of others. So how would it be if you jotted down your 12 favourite Old Testament stories? You could glance back on this chapter, allocate each to one of the traditions, and see which traditions are well represented. Then, ponder what to do next: are you only praying to an anthropomorphic God? Do you want to, or need to, broaden your experience of the mystical approach, say? Or if there are some stories that you know well but hate, you could see what needs to change for you to appreciate these afresh.

To complete the picture, we need not to ignore the quieter voices that emerge in some of the smaller books of the Old Testament: the common sense of Proverbs, the urbanity of Ecclesiastes, the scream of pain that is Job, and the ethereal beauty of Psalms and the Song of Solomon. All of these smaller books are rooted in the enterprise of faith that has already been described, but each leads us on in new directions, less limited to the people of Israel, more applicable in a universal context. The Old Testament is a classic collection of writings, in so many ways. The content and style of the Old Testament also creates new classics by requiring its readers to live in fresh ways as faithful disciples.

11

Addressing God

————•◦•————

When the Apartheid Museum opened in Johannesburg in 2001 it won many international awards for the balance of its design. The contractors had managed to find ways of presenting the story of apartheid and its overthrow that reconnected and inspired a wide range of visitors to the museum. Those who had suffered at the hands of the apartheid regime felt that the museum was telling and honouring their stories which had largely, under the regime, been ignored or hushed up. Many white South Africans who visited the museum, whether they had supported the regime or not, could follow the story of national pride, the mistreatment of a portion of their fellow citizens, and the emerging tales of redemption, restoration and reaching for a new identity. This is an inclusive museum which presents and holds together a wide variety of voices, challenging and confronting all those who visit.

When you buy an entrance ticket for the museum, you are given a receipt, a map and a small piece of card. The museum guard then directs those holding a piece of white card to the entrance on the left; those whose card is black are shown to the entrance on the right. The left-hand entrance is smart, comfortable and spacious; the door for those with the black cards is low, making you stoop as you enter. Once inside the museum, white-card holders and black-card holders are kept apart by a mesh fence that reaches to the ceiling. Each group is visible to the other, but between the two corridors a great gulf is fixed so that neither can cross over to the other side. Until the corridors meet in the first communal space, the museum embodies apartness, apartheid. Visitors from overseas, who may never had lived under the regime itself, enter the museum in the same way. So no one can view the museum without experiencing some of the truth and tales that it represents. Part of the offence that some visitors experience comes from the randomness of the allocation of white or black tickets at the very beginning. There is the feeling, 'I would have been on the other side', but for the chance allocation of a black/white ticket.

A church that wants to engage with a large proportion of its local community, and interact with many sections of the neighbourhood, needs to consider carefully how people want to enter. Being inclusive involves having many ways in that allow people to bring with them their dignity, their history and their conscience; being inclusive involves more than having a pleasant communal space, once people have entered. A friendly well-intentioned church can impose on outsiders the sort of entrances that the Apartheid Museum constructed which can be so off-putting, forcing people into behaviours that conflict with the fundamental values the church works to uphold.

This chapter explores a few consequences that flow from the language that is used about God, for this is one of the key ways into encounter with God. It is a commonplace that prayers written 400 years ago and Victorian hymns can be experienced as both indicative of the solemnity and enduring character of the faith, and also as irrelevant, out of touch and arcane. More than that, the way the Church speaks about God though traditional can be received as constraining and limiting. It can erect a mesh fence between those who value the tradition and those who, though wanting to engage with the Church, see their lives, their values and their intuitions of the divine in very different ways. Community engagement requires us to be more flexible in our use of language. This chapter will show that the Christian tradition, indeed, urges us in this direction as well. One crucial aspect of this is gender, and a touchstone for this is whether we refer to God as 'he', 'she' or 'it'.

The teacher was having a hard time explaining to her class that language matters and, in particular, that the gender-shape of our language is important. She explained and demonstrated how 'man' was once an inclusive term, encompassing men and women, but could no longer be assumed to be so now. Whatever the intentions of a speaker, 'man' is no longer routinely heard as the equivalent of 'human'. But the class was resistant. At a deep level they knew what was going on: that the teacher was not just giving them a history lesson, but was trying to persuade them to adopt a new perspective. They were enjoying their resistance and were pleased to see the increasing frustration and impotence of the teacher.

So she gave up. She passed on to other issues until, about 30 minutes later, she asked them to name ten of the most influential men in history. The class enjoyed this challenge, argued about whether bad leaders should be included in the list as well as those who had influenced the world for good, and eventually reduced the list to ten. On hearing the list she said, 'You have only given me names of men. What about women?' They were so quick to reply, 'But you only asked us for influential men' that they fell into her trap. Putting it simply, the class wanted in theory to use 'man' inclusively, but in practice they used it to refer only to males. Are we caught in a similar way with the word 'God'? We know that God should be seen to be beyond the image of 'a white man with a beard in the sky', yet we continue in practice only to refer to God as 'he' and with descriptions that are drawn largely from the experience of men.

How we begin to use words is important but does not determine everything. When teaching a child to pray, I want to stress the intimacy, kindness and gentle strength of God. The word 'God' itself may sound too stark, and so I will naturally use phrases such as 'Heavenly Father' or 'Our Father in heaven', authorized by Jesus himself. Jesus also used 'Abba', an Aramaic word best translated as 'my father' or 'dear father'. Praying with the same words as Jesus himself (though using a close equivalent in my natural language) expresses a profound connection, yet need not limit me. Nothing of what I want to explain in this chapter need challenge or undermine the tradition that we receive from Jesus. It would be a mistake too to see this exploration as founded solely in my own family history. Whereas I have a kind, patient, loving father, and a kind, patient, loving mother, the benefits I have found through varying the ways I address God are not rooted in my personal psychological development.

There are some ways of picturing the world that we develop so early in life that they become very deep-rooted. Indeed these patterns of thought become so ingrained that it is hard to imagine in other ways. I am probably not the only person who feels, at some profound level beyond the rational, that it is easier to drive south from Scotland to London than it is to drive north, for surely Scotland is uphill – *because it is at the top of the map*. In the playground as young children we may make jokes about those in Australia having to cling onto the earth otherwise they will fall off, or about them walking on their heads – *for surely they must be upright in the same way that we are*. And it is well known that the Arno Peters map of the world (devised as a new projection that more accurately correlated the area of the map with the surface area of the country) was initially not well received (and, indeed, rejected by some) for it disturbed an inner mental image.

Maps are one thing; the nature of God is another. Surely, some will say, God's nature, name and character is unchanging; this, they say, is the solid ground on which the whole Christian faith is based. Yet we do well to be careful about what we claim is eternally solid ground. I love to read articles in *National Geographic*, say, about plate tectonics. The illustrations are so

clear and informative, showing how the continents formed and
re-formed, describing how Spain was 'originally' part of South
America and how part of Scotland was once connected to
Australia. What we see now on a world map is merely the current arrangement of land masses. I wonder what it must have
been like for God, watching over millions and millions of years
the different patterns of what we like to call 'solid ground'.
I reckon God delights in that as much as she gently chuckles
over our insistence that our particular description of 'the divine'
must be true for all people in all times. A seminal theological
book, first published in 1968 and still challenging today, is *The
Christian Understanding of the Atonement* by F. W. Dillistone
which is essentially plate tectonics applied to the atonement;
over the centuries theologians described in different ways what
we need to be redeemed from, and explained in different ways
how salvation happens. What remains constant and reliable is
that, for the Christian, this only works with reference to Jesus
and, in particular, his death on the cross.

So our language about God can change without the whole
house of faith tumbling down. Indeed, as I have already hinted,
if we can be less enmeshed in our personal point of view and
see things *sub specie aeternitatis*, change is not only desirable
but also inevitable. What is particularly helpful for the story
that I am about to tell is that the Bible itself bears witness to
such change. Addressing God as 'she' is rooted in the biblical
record of how people of faith have addressed 'the Holy One'
over the centuries. There are three phases of this story.

First, when Abraham and Sarah left their homeland to travel
to Canaan (later to be known as Israel, 'the Promised Land'),
they believed they were called by God. But, which god? No community had yet developed a monotheistic faith; all worshipped
a variety of gods. The earliest biblical traditions use two different names: El and Yahweh. These names were recognized
across many tribes in the near Middle East, and were accepted
as being part of the 'host of heaven'.

The general view was that El was the oldest, originating father god who had been replaced as the chief god by Baal. This pattern we find in Roman and Greek mythology too when, for example, Zeus replaces Cronos as the chief god – the older god still lurks, though, in the background. In Canaan, Baal was a god associated with nature and the renewal of creation, and so (as in many cultures) there were stories of Baal's death and rebirth, associated with winter/spring. This seasonal transition was often marked in the temple by ritual sex acts between Baal and Ashteroth (one of the most common names of the senior goddess), and performed in reality between the priests and priestesses in the temple. It also seems that many tribes sacrificed the firstborn as a symbol of allegiance, including the sacrifice of the first male child.

Abraham's tribe began to differentiate themselves from the surrounding culture in two ways: they rejected child sacrifice (see Genesis 22), and they rejected temple sex. In the latter case, they therefore began to stand firmly against any female gods, or the inclusion of the feminine in the temple. That desire to be recognizably distinct from others is found so close to the origins of the history of our faith that it shapes spiritual expectations profoundly. Nevertheless Abraham's desire to belong to a distinctive community cannot determine how we today answer questions about the gender of God. We are dealing with a fundamentally different situation that involves us is finding how we can accept and appreciate female characteristics in God. I believe that when we do that, we naturally become more ready also to see what is godly in Christian women.

So the 12 tribes of Israel told stories based on two different names of God: El, the old originator, and Yahweh, portrayed as their tribal leader, a robust active strong god. Yahweh was still in those days seen as one among many but, as the centuries rolled by, Yahweh was increasingly seen as the challenger to Baal, eventually triumphing in battle against Baal and all his consorts. These stories were told just at the time the tribes of Israel were defeating the other tribes in Canaan. We can read about this in the older books in the Old Testament: Joshua, Judges, 1 and 2 Samuel, and 1 and 2 Kings, where the military victory of Israel is as much a theological victory of Yahweh over Baal.

Much of this will sound rather foreign and distant, but I remind you of this to make the point that we need to be careful about what conclusions we draw from this history. Whereas I am delighted that Abraham's tribe stopped child sacrifice, I don't have to adopt completely their vision of God as my own (not least because the understanding that there is only one God did not arise till much later).

Second, it was only after the people of Israel returned from their exile in Babylon (around 532 BC) that the vision of there only being one God really took root. Having tasted defeat in battle and having been banished from their land for generations, the Israelites become less wedded to an image of Yahweh as their tribal leader who guaranteed, and ruled in, their homeland. From the dust of defeat, the prophets brought forth a new vision of one God alone, a God of law, justice, right behaviour and righteousness. They still called this God 'Yahweh', but it was a very different Yahweh from the warrior god worshipped 500 years earlier. The tectonic plates were moving.

As the Israelites settled back in their homeland, weakened in their economy, social standing and political power, they increasingly spoke about God in terms that were not reserved for their tribes alone. A God who wanted people to live lives of honour, wisdom, peace, justice, nobility and compassion was a God who could be worshipped by everyone (whatever their culture) everywhere. This God (which we read of in the later books of the Old Testament, Proverbs, Psalms, and Job) was attractive to many in the Greek Empire. Ironically, just at the moment that the people of Israel were at their weakest, their religion became respected and admired around the Mediterranean.

The positive side of this is that new peoples were drawn into the faith of Yahweh, which is the foundation of our Christian tradition. The difficult question that had to be addressed was this: how much of the culture, teaching, traditions and rituals of the Israelites do I have to take on when I become a follower of Yahweh? The Greeks admired the teachings, but rather despised the old stories of the tribal gods. Thus we hear in the New Testament of Roman soldiers and Greeks who were supporters of the synagogue and prayed to Yahweh, but were not 'converted' into being 'fully paid up' Jews. After all, to this day, Judaism is not a faith of conversion but is something that is passed on through the family. This question was only finally addressed in the newly formed Christian communities by Paul (and not by Jesus), who claimed that the Gentiles who wanted to follow Christ did not first have to become Jews.

So once again, this history underlines the difficult issue of deciding what is an essential part of our faith, and what is a cultural expression. Just because the people of Israel did not recognize the female aspect of God for hundreds of years does not mean that we can't or shouldn't. A response that merely states, 'We should do as they did then' actually seems less than fully respectful to the way the Bible witnesses to a developing tradition.

Third, one further aspect of this changing image of God is visible in the later books of the Old Testament. The move away from a tribal god was also a move to a more settled, rational God. The literature (especially the book of Proverbs) focuses our attention on behaviour that is best articulated in straightforward rules which can be obeyed by everyone. Some of the psalms have that emphasis too: for example, Psalm 119, in which all 176 verses repeatedly point us to the rewards of keeping God's commandments, and the punishment of evil.

An endless diet of this can be soul-destroying. Ecclesiastes expresses that so well with its lament, 'There is nothing new under the sun.' A religion of pure morality is boring and uninspiring. It is likely that Job and the Song of Solomon were written in reaction against this. Job is a passionate shout of anger against a world based on 'The good are rewarded and succeed; but the bad are punished'. 'That's not true,' Job says against his comforters, who are typical of this rational and soulless religion. The book of Job finishes with the great claim that, even though bad things happen to good people, God is still with us, and accessible to us. The Song of Solomon is a book steeped in passion, longing, hope, intimacy and love – all of which can find little space within a religion based on morality.

Actually, there is one passage in Proverbs (the ultra-rational book) that shows the tradition correcting itself. Proverbs 8.22— 9.6 describes wisdom not simply as an attribute of God, but as part of God's own being. Wisdom is almost an embodiment of God; note the language: an 'embodiment', a 'putting into a body'. A rational God is a distinct, remote being, rather separate from our human condition. The scribes, in recognizing this, realized that the full truth of God was not being conveyed, so they felt drawn to describe God embodied as earthly Wisdom, present, active among us. Significantly, Sophia (the Greek word for wisdom) is feminine; there is a hint that when we meet God active here and now, we may need or choose to understand this using the feminine. Wisdom is not a part of God; Wisdom is a manifestation of God's true self.

So, three themes emerge as we focus on the shape of the faith as it changes over many generations:

- The revulsion felt against a female god was a positive development in the history of the Jewish spiritual tradition, but may not be completely relevant for us today;
- The Old Testament itself witnesses to a tradition that is dynamic in its understanding of God, recognizing new truths about God in new situations; and
- The moral side of our faith needs to be balanced by the passionate side, and this has been be done by using male and female imagery.

I wonder how you react to this story. Your personal and family history, combined with your experiences at work and with friends, may be sufficiently straightforward that the implications arising from the gendered nature of language neither interest nor concern you. But, to revert to the example of the Apartheid Museum, place yourself in the position of the museum guide who has to direct white-ticket holders one way and black-ticket holders another way. Is this forcing people into entrances that are unfair, random or inappropriate? Your response as a disciple might be that you are not troubled by these gender issues, but you recognize that others are. Working with the expectation of others is an essential part of community engagement.

I experienced this when visiting a local assault support centre. This is a small charity doing vital work with clients who have been deeply damaged. The clients need privacy, yet also want their stories to be heard and to be put in touch with resources for healing their past. It's a curious and tricky mix of desire for safe intimacy and public recognition. Equally, the charity was asking for a difficult mix: support, that would be accepted only on their terms. Financial support is relatively simple; knowing that they needed more space for interviewing clients, I offered temporary use of our church hall. They refused because for many of their clients there would be too many negative associations of the Church as an institution that is male, domineering, powerful and violent.

This may be felt to be unfair, but I have to take that experience seriously. How can we find ways, without jettisoning our tradition, of honouring this experience and an expressed desire to be connected to God who is the source of healing and restoration? Kindness and good will are necessary but not sufficient. It is important to be the sort of church that is confident in its tradition because that tradition is itself distinctive, dynamic and balanced. Phrasing this in a personal way, I may not need to change the way I pray, but I need to make it clear that other styles of prayer are valued and may cover some of my blind spots.

So perhaps the answer to 'Can we address God as "she"?' is the classic one: all can, some must, none should. That response allows variety, but requires each of us to consider deeply why we choose the path we do. Moreover, a consequence of having the freedom to choose the language of our praying is that we have to be cautious about imposing our choice on others. As a parish priest in the Church of England, I am required 'only to use the forms of service as authorized by Canon'. In other words, I cannot simply make up forms of worship as I wish, yet, by implication, the Church recognizes that there are services that are unauthorized. Equally, St Paul did not sit down one day and decide to write a bit of the New Testament; he wrote a letter to his friends in Corinth which, after much use and discernment, was named as worthy of being included in the Bible. Tradition without explanation is mere history.

A few years ago this parish decided to test out this pattern of praying publicly. We compiled a service that intentionally drew on feminine imagery and names for God and her activity among us. We changed some of the actions in the service as well as the words so that there was a freshness to what we did as well as what we said. The visiting preacher was magnificent. I was much relieved that the bishop chose not to call in unannounced that Sunday. In the reflections afterwards, there was no complaint. One person wanted reassurance that we could still say the Lord's Prayer in 'the' traditional form. But what everyone really loved was the new way that the offertory was presented at the altar, with the prayer said by the people, not the priest; that was the truly inclusive moment. By paying attention to the language we used, we inadvertently stumbled across a new action which affirmed what we were really after: the acceptability of our personal offerings by God. Language changes behaviour. Yes, we need courage to explore; but perhaps there will be times, while we are attempting to find new paths, it will not feel strange, because what we are doing is so right.

12

Finding another way

———•◦•———

As we consider how to be creative disciples today, the emphasis on community engagement, which is a theme running through this book, affects not only what we do but also what we say. The language and examples we use to talk about our faith will change if we always have in mind those who may not themselves be believers. Even when participating in internal church discussions, it can be useful to have a chair (literally or metaphorically) set aside for your neighbour down the street who displays no interest whatever in church life. Taking care with language is important and is something that you will experience if interviewed for radio. You cannot rely on visual aids, hand gestures or eye contact; all the listener can hear is your language, yet they will sense your attitudes that are heard within the words you use.

Many people have a love/hate relationship with the media. We hate the way stories are polarized and differences exaggerated. Often journalists will seek to tell a more exciting story by dividing all the participants into two camps. This does not sit well with the classic Church of England attitude of 'both/and' rather than 'either/or'. Whereas some in the Church of England still call themselves Protestants, the image and attitude of being a person who is permanently protesting leaves something to be desired. Yet those who are approached for an interview on radio love the opportunity to tell their tales. The discipline which is imposed on speakers who honour this emphasis of positive engagement with the community requires speakers to be comprehensible (without using jargon) and accessible (without being bland).

Internal ecclesiastical squabbles damage and discredit both sides. Listening to a person who is passionate about something trivial and irrelevant can call the whole enterprise of faithful living into disrepute. A useful tool that can lever speakers out of such irrelevancies is called 'appreciative discourse' and is applicable in many different circumstances. For example, if I want to say something negative about a proposal set before a committee in a business meeting, I have to be prepared to name four things I appreciated about the proposal before I criticize it. Naming four can be a real challenge. The very minimum is to name one positive before each negative, but that pattern only seems to emphasize the polarization: good/bad maps on to me/ you. In having to name three positives first about a proposal that I dislike I have often found that I contribute to the whole group understanding a proposal better, including strengths and weaknesses. The latter hardly need to be named if the former are properly articulated.

This chapter touches on some of the themes that can be profoundly divisive in church life: the nature of biblical inspiration, the location of God's revelation, and how Scripture can be used today. The chapter tries to find new ways of visualizing these theological issues that are sensitive to the feelings that 'conservatives' and 'liberals' (to use the unhelpfully polarized terms) can have. Yet the emphasis is on images that can be used as we talk with communities outside the Church about the inspiration of the Bible and the presence of God now.

The North Downs straddle a beautiful ridge that runs on an east–west axis just south of London. At midday the views looking southwards are archetypal of great English countryside. Gentle rolling hills provide valleys in which villages snuggle, and viewpoints are often topped with a semaphore tower, used in the eighteenth century for passing messages from Portsmouth to London. From my vantage point on one hill, I can imagine what it would be like to stand on the next hill, and so the countryside stimulates imagination. Acres of trees are pierced by clearings, so there is often a sense of half-hiddenness, that there is always more to be revealed beyond the next field.

Since our new puppy needs many walks each day, I have recently learnt to enjoy the downs at sunrise too. I love walking westwards just as the new day's light catches the trees. In the gloom the wood edging the field looks a dusty green, yet it catches fire at the moment of sunrise. Each day the miracle of the burning bush is repeated: this place burns with glory yet is not consumed. The view is wonderful at any time of day; but at sunrise, it is *seen* to be wonderful. The sun's rays, quite literally, bring to light a beauty that, just a few minutes before, existed but was not apparent.

Walking eastwards at this time of day is a different experience. I appreciate the moment just before dawn as a time of potential; I can feel that a new creation is about to begin. Facing east, as the sun rises, the view becomes darker. The hedgerows, that a moment before appeared dark green, now seem black with the sun's rays behind them; the silhouettes of trees, spires and chimneys are marvellous. The brilliance of the sun, even a few seconds after its rising, is too much to look at. Walking east, you see with great clarity: there are lines; some shapes are black and others bright. Walking west, you enjoy the 'bringing to light'. You cannot face both ways at once. I am a west-facing person myself. I want to see the beauty around me that is revealed by the sun's rays coming from behind me.

I resist those voices in the Church that seem to tell me only to face the Son. This is a powerful approach to faith which promises clarity, well-defined boundaries, and makes what is light brilliant and what is grey very black. But I reckon that I am not alone in feeling that my soul withers if I am forced only to look eastwards. I believe passionately in the importance of Jesus Christ, and in the active presence of God's Spirit of holiness, and in the significance of the witnesses recorded in the Bible. Yet I have experienced a long spiritual journey to feel confident in these beliefs while still looking westwards (in a spiritual sense), and have been dismayed to see others, after their initial enthusiasm for the faith, burnt up and burnt out by only facing east.

Part of that journey for me has been to turn one particular Bible verse from a weapon used against me into a friend: 2 Timothy 3.16 says 'all Scripture is inspired by God'. How many times did I hear in my teenage years talks that began with that verse and moved subtly to 'only Scripture is inspired by God' to 'only Scripture is perfect knowledge, completely accurate and is insulted if challenged'! Now, after learning to resist these subtle over-elaborations of the verse, I can take great comfort in this text. Paul encourages his readers to be alert to God's breathing life and strength into them as Scripture is read. The following verse is remarkably inclusive: all who belong to God will be equipped for good work. The focus is no longer back to Scripture but is on the disciple, bouncing on the springboard of Scripture, ready to dive forwards into good work, being 'proficient' and trained 'in righteousness'.

I am reminded of the tale of Michael, which I was told many years ago. Michael loved his work but was slowly going blind. So he moved house to live close enough to his workplace to walk there each day. He was given a guide dog which he loved. All went well for the first few months because the guide dog was intelligent and the journey was not too hard to learn: three blocks, turn left; two blocks, cross the river; turn right; and then a few hundred yards on the left was his office. One day Michael was worried because the dog led him by a slightly different route. There was enough trust between dog and master that Michael did not try to steer the dog (for he too could envisage the route clearly) – perhaps there were roadworks, as the pavement was dug up? But when Michael arrived at the office no one could recall that there was anything the dog had intentionally avoided. The same thing happened on the way home and the next morning. By this time Michael, trusting the dog and recognizing that he was still achieving everything he wanted (namely, to get from home to office safely, and back again), supposed that the dog was bored. The dog knew what to do and how to do it – and now wanted to branch out. In the end the dog eventually learned about all the different bridges across the river and enjoyed a different route home each day.

I wonder sometimes whether God gets bored and longs for us to be a bit more adventurous. With trust on both sides, we will be protected from harm and evil. The line from the hymn 'Abide with me' has a lot to answer for:

> Change and decay in all around I see;
> O thou who changest not, abide with me.

As I sing that, I remember Michael and his trusting, confident, intelligent, faithful dog. I wonder whether the title 'Thou who changest not' is sufficient or accurate for God. It would be easy to see the theme of this chapter as a tussle between two approaches: conservative and liberal, facing east and facing west. But 'has been revealed' and 'is being revealed' are not opposites. The dog could not experiment without having first learnt the most straightforward route. Equally, learning a clear route is good initial foundation, but may not be the best use of talent for ever after.

So the first image in this chapter (walking in the North Downs) stresses that you cannot face east and west at the same time: choose and enjoy the different views. Whereas the second image (the guide dog who was bored) stresses faithful development and trust. Lurking between these two stories is a desire to be honest about valuing the spiritual tradition that forms us and about what it may require of us today. The link between past revelation and present action is important and must be maintained. It is inadequate to read the Bible with the attitude: 'Once I've read it, then I can move on to the difficult business of living faithfully today.' The shape of a traditional sermon that moves only from Bible to application can actually collude with a devaluing of the past, the Bible being seen as something that we are always moving away from. So, here is another image.

I was fascinated to read that Venice is founded on clay. All the classic photos of Venice will show it as a city floating on water, not rooted on solid ground at all. But actually Venice is settled on clay *under which* is fresh water. Though there is water everywhere in Venice (and, often, too much), this is salt water. Without the fresh water underneath the clay the city would never survive. So the earliest builders drilled down to sink pipes that provide fresh water, which is still accessible from the wells that are the centrepieces of many public courtyards. What gathers people together is the drawing of fresh water. This is the necessary link that largely remains invisible. Putting it starkly: the Bible is too important to leave to conservatives; liberals have to show how they draw 'living water' from the true spiritual source that remains largely hidden and how that can be a public enterprise. But I want to refrain from simplifying increasingly acrimonious church debates into a struggle between two camps. Indeed, Venice knows very well about the need to reconcile opposites. The city wants to stop the tides washing away the soil that provides its foundations; yet the city needs the tides to wash away the stagnant water. Every honest tradition seeks to be both rooted and refreshed by the swirling tides of God's love.

Perhaps one way of looking at the issue I am dealing with is to ask: where do we locate God's inspiration? There are two classic responses that I believe are inadequate: one is to locate all inspiration in the past (and a simple interpretation of 2 Timothy 3.16 does just that); the other is to acknowledge two eras of faithful living: the golden age of biblical times and now. Those familiar with reading church reports will recognize the latter approach, which often have, say, three chapters setting out the biblical and theological material, followed by three chapters on 'what we should do now'. There is often little to link the two halves of the report, and seldom anything about how faithful Christians responded in the intervening centuries. Church history did not stop in AD 100 (roughly when the Bible was completed), only to start again in 1950. The overwhelmingly positive reaction to Diarmaid MacCulloch's *A History of Christianity* is perhaps testimony to a desire to understand and recognize the many strands that connect us to our past. Theologically, this reminds us that God's inspiring Spirit is to be located in all places and through all times, even though the behaviour that was inspired then may not be appropriate for today.

There is an icon in St Catherine's Monastery, Sinai, which holds together in one picture a number of answers to the question of where God's inspiration is to be located. At first sight, the icon is about St John composing his Gospel. The halo around John's head reminds us of his holiness and God's presence in his life. Above, there is the image of a dove: the Spirit being sent from heaven to overshadow John. On the other side of the icon, there is the figure of Prochorus, who is traditionally regarded as John's scribe. The figure appears to balance that of the Evangelist. So inspiration is to be located in the hearing and recording as well as in the original speaking. In the centre of the icon there a table; on this you can see the manuscript on which Prochorus is writing, thus affirming the importance of the written text. Yet, if you look closely you can see that the manuscript holds the words (in English translation): 'In the beginning was the Wo . . .' The look on John's face is that of 'How shall I put this?' The icon seems to be affirming that the text is still in the process of being composed (even in our own day), and so warns us against closing down the period of inspiration. Finally, underneath the table, you can see some rolled-up parchment – as yet unused – implying that there is more inspiration still to come. This icon brilliantly affirms God's inspiration, past, present and future – God's presence above us, in us, and in those we affect by the words which we speak today.

With this emphasis on the continuing presence of God among us, I would now be happy to say that I believe in angels. I was reintroduced to this term through a completely secular book that helped me prepare to run a marathon. After many chapters about training, the closing chapter offered guidance for the race-day itself, with good advice about wearing the right shoes and kit, and taking enough water. At the end, it simply said, 'Look for your running angel.' There will be someone who is the right person for you, doing the right thing at the time you most need it. But running angels don't wear wings or halos. As we gathered at the start line, I was looking around the vast crowd, wondering where my angel would be. The gun went, and we slowly surged away; the excitement made thoughts of angels vanish. I knew that one of the key tactics to running a good marathon is to settle into the right pace. So, in the early miles, I was concentrating on that when I looked up for a moment to see the same runner ten metres ahead. He'd been there for a little while – I remembered the race number on his back. Initially I didn't want to become too attached to him and his pace, for you can make a big mistake by running at a pace that is just too fast or just too slow for your own body. But after ten minutes, I realized that he was moving at exactly the right speed for me, and he was my running angel. He carried me round for 20 miles, no wavering on pace, always ten metres ahead. Voicelessly he kept me going as I flagged, and held me back as I got my second wind. I lost sight of him at mile 22 but shouted, 'Thank you' as I felt his presence leave me. In my parish work I meet 'ministry angels': those whose path through life helps keep me on track, often because, unknown to me, they have themselves received encouragement from my ministry. The attitude that is needed is one of trust in the presence and connectedness of God, some of which is made visible in the Church.

We live in an enchanted world that is super-saturated with God's grace. Angels are probably all around us even if sometimes they take the bodily form of a sweaty 50-year-old man trudging around a 26-mile marathon route. Many live with a low level appreciation of this: they recognize the truth but cannot put it into words. One of the roles that a faithful disciple can have is to be the sort of person who can take the moment to condense God's grace into actions so that it can be seen, heard and spoken about by others. Gerard Manley Hopkins writes: 'The world is charged with the grandeur of God'; disciples are people where inspiration happens and who make grandeur become visible. It is a shame to live in such a glorious world without being aware of it. The consciousness of grace matters.

When our old dog, Treacle, died the family was very sad. As part of our bereavement, we vacuumed the house thoroughly and tidied away her toys. We needed to feel her absence. A few months later we welcomed a new puppy into our house. She was showered with love and a new beginning was made. Yet I became aware that, for the puppy, our house must be infused with many signs of a dog's presence: bite marks on the furniture, scratches on the door, smells on the dog towel. The puppy inhabits our house as a world, rich in signals of dogginess yet without a canine companion. I can't put this into words for her: that she is loved now, that she is part of an ongoing habit of loving dogs, and that one day she will leave behind her traces for the next dog to puzzle over. I can't do that for my puppy; but perhaps all disciples can do that for each other. This chapter has been, in part, an elaboration of a phrase which is currently in vogue: 'Let us find out what God is doing and join in.' George Caird says roughly the same in his hymn 'Not far beyond the sea', where he reminds us of the living presence of God's Word. As we journey onwards, further light and truth will be given to us.

Offering these personal examples in a spiritual reflection on the importance of the Bible is intended to stimulate your own creativity. It may be that my images resonate sufficiently with you that they become your own too. But the emphasis must be on each disciple finding words to convey how the Bible works and what happens when it does. The year 2011 was the four-hundredth anniversary of the translation of the Authorized Version. During that year there were many moving services and radio programmes based on fresh individual voices speaking about how a particular verse had become a condensed presence of God's Word. Consider this: a journalist puts a microphone under your nose and asks:

> The Bible is in flames. You can save for posterity one verse. What would it be? How does this verse connect you with the faith you have inherited and the future for which you hope? How can you describe that in a way that your neighbour becomes excited too?

13

A foot in both camps

When preparing for a journey it is good to know not only your destination and route, but also what sort of journey you are undertaking. This chapter seeks to understand more clearly what sort of exploration is being undertaken as disciples engage positively, in particular, with the world of work. The phrase 'pioneer ministry', much loved in the Church today, conjures up an image of valiant ministers crossing a frontier. Such pioneers leave behind the safety of their homeland, and support of fellow believers, to go into territory which, by implication, lacks the civilizing presence of the gospel or, indeed, is hostile to it. Some pioneers, to change the image slightly, see themselves as entering territory that is blank, empty of values or worthwhile history, with people who have no ready-formed attitude towards the gospel for it has never been part of their lives. The use of the term 'pioneer' is good for recruitment as it taps into these exciting images; but I wonder how realistic such images are, and whether they correlate at all with the behaviour and attitudes of those on the receiving end of such ministry.

Perhaps the sort of exploration that falls to many disciples is more realistically described as travelling within one's home-land, among people who speak the same language (largely). There is a valid ministry that involves making connections with those among whom you already live. This discipleship involves bridge-building. It involves interpreting; this is not translating the gospel from 'church language' into a new language for people who have never heard of it in their own tongue, but is rather based on bringing experience into the vernacular. The skills that are required are those of a facilitator who (literally) makes it easy for others to recognize patterns and identify what pieces of their experience are most significant. I am reminded of images of the days when cities had to endure 'pea-souper' fogs: no one could see much more than a few feet in front of their noses. Such a city needs guardians who act as signposts ('This is the way, follow it', as in Isaiah 30), or who walk in front of buses waving a red flag ('Beware, stand aside, so you are not damaged'), or who are sufficiently familiar with the fog-drenched streets that they can take those who are lost at least part of the way home, handing them over to other guardians for the rest of their journey. There is much in this image that, I believe, correlates more fully with what our culture and nation need today, and what the Church as a whole, and disciples as individuals, can offer.

These two contrasting images are closely aligned with two contrasting aspects of church work, each of which has associated with it an old (but barely understood) title: catechesis and apologetics. Catechesis refers to the process of the Church teaching those who do not know the traditions, beliefs, behaviours and worship patterns of the Christian faith. The work of evangelists and catechists goes hand in hand: the former starts the process, the latter takes it to 'Stage 2'. But thinking about mission in this way is so often done with the underlying image that I described earlier in this chapter: those on the receiving end are hostile, or lack previous knowledge, or are blank slates on which the Church can engrave its values. 'Apologetics', on the other hand, refers to the process of making sense of, or giving reasons for, or explaining in terms that suit the listener, the Christian gospel. For this approach apologetics is Stage 2, connecting is Stage 1. A timid church that is concerned about its home-base and falling numbers of supporters, or feels threatened by the surrounding culture, can delight in the pioneer image. It takes confidence and courage to walk out into the fog and see how you can be a guardian angel for the city in which you live. This is what we seek to understand better in this chapter.

I want to introduce you to two priests, each of whom is in full-time secular employment, each of whom is actively involved in ministry and discipleship in the fog of their working lives as well as helping in a part-time capacity in their respective parishes. By using Ann and James as my examples I am not implying that this sort of ministry is limited to the ordained alone. Being ordained, as you will see, may be the catalyst for some of what happens; it provides the excuse and occasion for some conversations; it provides visibility (at times). But all that Ann and James do 'in the fog' can be done by any lay disciple too. Indeed I give these examples to indicate the paths that are there for all disciples to travel.

James is the chief operating officer for an engineering firm, who is often required to be on the front line, winning new business for his firm. We meet him first as he stands at the bar at the end of a day's conference, informal time. On his left is the managing director of a firm which, James hopes, is about to place a contract with James, who is doing all he can to impress. On his immediate right is a junior colleague of the MD who, having heard that James is an engineer and a priest, is fascinated by this dual role and wants to talk about the Church. In the nature of noisy bars, James cannot move to a quieter corner with either person; he feels he has to keep both conversations going at the same time, in a loud enough way that means that each partner can listen in to the other's conversation. Integrity is crucial – both within the religious chat, and to impress the boss, and also there has to be integrity between both conversations. James says that such integrity is formed and nourished by praying regularly over an extended period for his work. The prayer is not that God would make James' firm prosper (though that is a valid hope), but that James can naturally and automatically visualize God as present in this firm. To help achieve this, James says Morning Prayer at his desk. The goal is that James can speak to the MD and the junior colleague at the same time without compromising either conversation.

Ann works in a very different environment. She is a finance officer in local government which, though a public service, has its own culture that imposes many constraints on all employees. This culture struggles with visible signs of religion, so Ann has never worn her dog collar to work. At Ann's ordination, her guests were mainly family and neighbours with only a few special and close friends from work. It could have been awkward and inappropriate to invite her whole work team to this special ordination day, however well she got on with her colleagues. Although some Christians rather easily see themselves as under persecution, this is not a culture of hostility, merely a culture of restraint. So Ann's priestly ministry at work is largely one of influence and character. The challenge to live a valid ministry largely without using words is huge. Yet I recognize that my ministry as a parish priest is made easier because people like Ann are the bridges over which others can travel to come to church.

Both Ann and James agree that, although the culture of their workplaces does not make public faith easy, there are some conversations that would never take place were they not known as representatives of the Church. Ordination short-circuits some of these difficulties, but any disciple can be seen to be a representative provided the right attitude is carried within. Both have noted that many conversations are occasioned by a death. People want funeral advice, ranging from how to deal with undertakers to how to deal with their own families, split by divorce or painful disagreements. Even more fog descends at the time of death as so many of the traditional paths through the difficulties of bereavement are unknown or unvalued in our culture. This is where a disciple having a little professional knowledge, a lot of confidence and the wisdom to wave a warning flag over some issues can be enormously helpful. But there are moments when the water-cooler conversation becomes very sensitive. James was asked for help by a colleague whose closest friend had just died in her mid-40s, leaving two children. In the end James agreed that he would himself write a letter to these children along the lines of 'Where is God when a good person dies?' The widower replied some weeks later: 'I am not a church-goer, but if I were, yours would be the church I would come to.' It would be hard (and maybe inappropriate) for James to pursue this contact, but a bridge has been created and some other parish priest may see someone crossing it in some years' time.

Ann has experience of making valuable connections that are dependent on, but not based at, her workplace. Having visited HIV projects in Africa, she wanted to mark World Aids Day, not only for her church but also for her town. It was easy for Ann to send appropriate invitations, and for people to respond, because she was known in the networks of local health and public service professionals. What she was doing, stemming from her personal experience and beliefs, rang true with others. Ann invited a wide range of people from the health service, charities, clinics, churches and clients to an event – this was not a service, but a moment for conversations, candle-lighting, remembrance, mutual valuing and support. The bridge-building meant that this occasion was not liturgical, but the invitation, the approach, and the one doing the inviting all cohered to create a safe space which moved people deeply.

Even though disciples may take the initiative to build bridges, as in creating the World Aids Day event, both Ann and James have recognized that those they meet want these bridges to be created. James had to fly at short notice to Vietnam just before Christmas to settle a new contract. He was waiting to be interviewed by the main board of directors of the firm that was to hire him, in a room with his counterpart, the person who was recommending James and his firm. This man had studied James' CV as well as reading the tender document, and so knew James was a priest. Both sat still, silent and nervous, before the final interview began. Suddenly the Vietnamese spoke: 'Why are atheists so angry? Especially in our city culture today we need more peace and space. Atheists don't allow the first and restrict the second.' How do you reply to that, just as you are composing yourself to win a new piece of business? The tone was clear: James' colleague, a Buddhist, assumed and relished that they had much in common; he spoke about enjoying Christmas as a Buddhist: 'We need all the opportunities that we can get to show people that we love them.' While James was still struggling to keep up with this conversation, he was called in for the interview to hear the first remark: 'Your CV tells me you have a theology degree. I want to hire an engineer. But perhaps you are just searching for truth in different ways.' The bridges we need to build are ones that allow two-way traffic.

What lies at the heart of this way of being a disciple that is located essentially in the workplace? It seems to involve three key elements:

- the disciple being a person who can recognize moments of significance and not let them pass by;
- the disciple who is multilingual, being able to interpret people and situations in ways that are easily heard by others;
- the disciple as an 'occasion-er', a person who makes things happen or whose presence turns the commonplace into a time of revealing.

I imagine that you will be involved in these sorts of times when you will feel you are on the edge of something weighty. Recognizing them and being ready to talk about them with friends is important. That requires wisdom and confidence. But there is something more, as yet unsaid, that is about having the sort of character that makes you a disciple around whom these special moments happen. What helps form this sort of character?

As I look at Ann and James I see two people who are ready to communicate. James is a good talker, Ann is a good listener; the latter characteristic can be an essential part of a good occasion as much as the former. You will know that a disgruntled teenager may be helped by being given a good 'listening to' rather than a good 'talking to'. The Benedictine vow of obedience involves a monk in learning to be a person who listens profoundly, the Latin words for 'obey' and 'hear' being very similar. A person who is humble enough to listen well is also likely to be a person who knows where good resources are to be found. The World Aids Day event was such a success because Ann had connected people and helped them find in each other some of the resources needed to continue in their several struggles.

When this small group met and found themselves participating in a grace-rich moment, Ann asked them to do three simple and basic actions. They were asked to name what they were grateful for. You will probably know how a naturally grateful person can bring light and energy into a room. Gratitude is a great radiator, and not a drain. They were asked to say sorry. The detail of the 'confession' probably did not matter as much as being asked to participate honestly, recognizing our fallibility is another way to release energy. They were asked to name the help they wanted (not necessarily for other members present), which is closely connected to naming what they hoped for.

These elements fit together not least because they are all part of what it is to be prayerful. A disciple who prays is one who is keen to talk and listen to God, one who is ready to look for reasons beyond himself or herself, one who is regularly grateful, one who is comfortable with saying sorry, and one who creates hope by taking the first step towards it. When any disciple prays in this fashion over an extended period, Christian character is being moulded in a way that others recognize and to which they will respond. There is an ancient proverb that says: 'You make paths by walking.' When disciples walk this way, confident that God is forming their character as they journey on, they will find they are accompanied by others, whether in need or of goodwill. That is a reminder that this chapter is not about what a super disciple can do, excusing us of our responsibilities. All disciples have a foot in both camps.

14

Experiencing resurrection

From the start of this book the importance of vicarious living has been emphasized. The Church acts out the faith on behalf of the nation. Congregations are faithful, in part, on behalf of their local communities. Individuals will speak out vicariously for their congregations. This pattern of faithful living on behalf of others brings many benefits as we gain strength in times of difficulties, we see guiding lights in times of personal darkness and learners (disciples) can be accompanied by those who have trodden the path before. One of the main dangers of such vicarious living is often called 'group-think' and is best described in the story of the emperor's new clothes. It is possible for a whole group to kid themselves and play along with a belief that does not square with their experience. When no one has the courage to name the dissonance between their words and experience, the whole group can be deluded and so damaged. The danger of 'We believe' is that individually and privately each person is thinking: '. . . but I don't; nevertheless I'll go along with my tribe.'

A tribe can avoid this danger if it truly treasures individual voices. Any tribe may claim it does this, but energy and effort is required to honour disruptive voices. We need prophets who disturb us, poets who paint word-pictures in brighter tones than we are used to, and leaders who afflict the comfortable (as well as comforting the afflicted). Any congregation or church that does not at times hear discordant voices in their delibera-tions is likely not to be serving its community well for it will only be living vicariously for a segment of the population. This part of the book has been written in the belief that the Bible and tradition encourage us to trust that unified and varied exploration into the mystery of God is possible.

Another mechanism for avoiding the danger of vicarious living is to ensure that 'We believe' is regularly translated into 'I believe'. What belongs to the community, present or past, must be routinely made personal as well. If the communal is reduced to the personal, then a congregation becomes merely individuals who happen to be in the same room. This book has emphasized the importance of communal faith. At the close, it is right to safeguard that by underlining the importance of personal faith as well.

St Aldate's Church in Oxford stands in the mainstream of the evangelical tradition. It has long had a lively influential ministry in the city, especially among students. Many have experienced there, as I did, deep Christian friendship, a call to active service in this world, and powerful preaching. It is nearly 30 years since I last attended that church but I can still recall the emphasis that was placed on the three classic parts of that theological tradition: the inerrancy of the Bible, the atoning sacrifice of Christ on the cross, and a need for personal conversion. Though comfortable with this basic structure, in this book I have been encouraging us to explore and experiment with the tradition. I would prefer to name the Bible as trustworthy rather than inerrant. Christ's death is crucial, but I would want to explore a number of images that describe how the cross connects us with the power and presence of God. In this chapter, I am exploring the third element: personal conversion. Nothing I say will challenge the huge importance of this. Much as I have been affirming the significance of corporate discipleship, this does not diminish the need and excitement of personal change as we become ever more closely connected with the life of God.

Revelation 3.20 is a classic text for a sermon on conversion: 'Listen! I am standing at the door, knocking; if you hear my voice and open the door, I will come in to you and eat with you, and you with me.' In the right context, that is a moving, challenging image which beckons us to respond. But at other times, and for some who find themselves on their spiritual and emotional journeys at a less well-defined junction, conversion can be a matter of a dawning awareness. R. S. Thomas, in his poem, 'The Bright Field', describes beautifully the experience of being touched momentarily by grace, yet in a way that starts a pursuit of God's treasure which can last a lifetime. Conversion can also be a matter of finding your ultimate companion; this sounds like marriage and the analogy with the process of finding a partner, making a life commitment and embarking upon a shared journey is intentional. For this pattern, a conversion sermon might be based on Ephesians 3 ('being rooted and grounded in love') or 2 Corinthians 5 ('the love of Christ leaves us no choice' (NEB)). Whatever approach is taken, two elements are being recognized and joined: that God actively calls me personally, and that I willingly (with all my will) respond and commit. As I describe this, I am not wanting to channel anyone into replicating my experience. Just the opposite! But I have come to believe that there is something about discipleship that inescapably involves us in no longer merely being a messenger, but we are people who experience the life of God first-hand. Disciples do not merely retell 'the old, old story' but relate what is happening now. We are responsible not only for reporting but also for creating the message, as God's Spirit is active here and now.

There is a touching tale about a moment of partial understanding, of knowing all the main ingredients but not yet experiencing the whole truth directly. This tale, if not wholly accurate, deserves to be true. Bradley Wiggins, a great British cyclist, was racing in the Tour de France. There were high expectations that he would do well, so it was a tragedy when he crashed out, breaking some bones. As Wiggins had to spend a lot of time away from home because of his profession, he wanted to phone his young children as soon as he got out of hospital to tell them the news, for they were just getting to the age of being enthusiastic about cycling. He phoned them, but was interrupted before he started speaking by his excited son. 'Daddy, Daddy, I've been watching the Tour de France. Do you know? Bradley Wiggins has crashed out of the race!' How touching! The young boy loves cycling; he loves his father; he admires Bradley Wiggins – but he had not quite connected all three of these together. He was not yet able to equate Bradley Wiggins with Daddy.

A few years ago, Eric James, a great preacher and then a regular contributor to 'Thought for the Day' on Radio 4, visited Guildford early in January on the festival day known as 'the baptism of Christ'. For his sermon, he took as his text the painting of Christ's baptism by Piero della Francesca. It was magisterial: the preacher describing the subtleties of the painting as well as linking the theology of baptism, incarnation and discipleship. The congregation were on the edge of their seats. I can remember it clearly, as I can also recall feeling that the final ingredient was left unspoken: 'And what about *you*?' I could not tell whether the preacher had pulled this final punch, or had wanted to leave it unspoken. The central theme of the sermon was 'intersection': heaven meeting earth, God in Christ, water and Spirit. But when, I wanted to know, are you going to ask *us* to be the place of intersection too?

Still, the sermon had a powerful effect, for I became fascinated by Piero della Francesca's work. So when I was on holiday in northern Italy a few years later, I knew I had to take the opportunity to go and see his painting of the Resurrection. On the evening before, I read the guidebook which recounts the remarkable story about how this painting was preserved during the Second World War. As the allied forces advanced through Italy, the Germans slowly retreated town by town. One German detachment made its base one evening in the hill town of Sansepolcro. The British officer laid plans that night to fire his artillery into the town in the morning so that he could more readily capture it. But when he asked the gunnery officer the name of the town, a vague memory was stirred. The officer too turned to an old guidebook to find that it claimed that the most beautiful painting in the world was located in this village. Moreover, the painting was a fresco, painted directly on to a wall, and so could not be moved. Early in the morning he sent a message in to the town inviting the Germans to leave, giving them time to withdraw gracefully and safely, so that lives would not be lost and the painting would be saved. Fortunately, they agreed. As I read this story, 60 years later, I was so moved that I knew I wanted to be part of it. Seeing the painting would somehow connect me to that remarkable story.

As I drove to Sansepolcro, I was aware, as you are, of the layers upon layers in this moment: a story about a story, recounted in books, vaguely recalled. Yet as I walked into the Museo Civico, I was floored, for walking towards me was Christ. Piero della Francesca's skill is so great that the risen Christ appears to be in front of the painting, stepping out towards the onlooker. The sleeping Roman soldiers are the background; the empty tomb is the foreground. In front of this, seemingly walking out of the wall and into the room is the risen Christ. In the role of art critic, I had to go up to the wall to check that the painting was indeed two-dimensional. But, as a believer, I had experienced resurrection.

As I stood there in amazement, two verses from the book of Job came to mind. The first is a verse made famous by the aria in Handel's oratorio *Messiah*: 'I know that my Redeemer lives, and that at the last he will stand upon the earth . . . in my flesh I shall see God . . . my eyes shall behold, and not another' (Job 19.25–27). At this stage Job knows a truth, but acknowledges that only some time later will he actually experience it. The second verse is the climax of the whole book, and the fulfilment of what had been up till then second-hand knowledge. At the end Job declares: 'I had heard of you by the hearing of the ear, but now my eye sees you' (Job 42.5). The tragic journey of Job is completed as he finally is connected with the God that he, until then, had spoken about but not met. Job's counsellors had misled him and betrayed the truth of God. But in the end what matters is not the dismissal of false counsellors; rather it is the personal, immediate, direct connection with God.

A classic line used by many theatre directors when addressing their actors is: 'Play the text, not the interpretation of the text'. Of course, any performance is an interpretation. But the temptation is strong to act an interpretation rather than live the text as given. Actors must play Shakespeare; disciples are called to live the gospel, not an interpretation of the gospel. Being part of a tradition, whether theatrical or spiritual, makes one aware of how people have lived their text in previous generations. Actors or disciples who are unaware or dismissive of what has gone before are either arrogant or dangerous. Humility requires us both to acknowledge our inheritance and to dare to create a fresh performance ourselves. Personal commitment is too important a matter only to tell others about; we have to live it authentically ourselves. 'We believe' and 'I believe' nurture and enhance each other. The image of a jug and wine may be illuminating. The tradition is the jug, holding what must be fresh and consumed, thereby itself creating memories of happiness and refreshment. As well as that, I am the jug, hollowed out and moulded to preserve and present the vintage from the past. So speaking of resurrection is not only about proclaiming future hope and present experience, it also involves connecting with the God who is the origin of everything.

How can I speak to you about Easter without talking also about the beginning of the world? In Genesis 1 we read that God commands light, and light happens. God commands sun, moon, earth, land and humans; and they all happen. As this poetic chapter advances, you can feel the power bursting forth. There may also be darkness but that does not stop the light.

There may be difficulties in heaven (see also Revelation 12.7 'and war broke out in heaven'), but that does not stop God's *shalom*. There may be tragedy on earth, but that does not stop an energetic, creative, commanding God. This is a God, who from the beginning, spits in the face of death: 'I created, and I can re-create.' Easter makes sense as a continuation of this powerful life that is our beginning and the beginning of all of creation. I cannot prove this to you; I can state that it happened and encourage you to look for signs today. So when the risen Jesus appears to Mary in the garden on the first Easter Day, his word is a word of command: 'Mary! I am back; come with me.'

As you know, Genesis contains two stories of the Creation. So, Easter must also be connected with the gentler, more tender narrative, contained in Genesis 2. There we are given a picture of God as our companion, a God who sits alongside us, asking quietly of each new animal that emerges: 'What shall we call this one?' This is a God who understands us and brings us new treasures to enrich our lives. This is a God to whom we can admit our pain, our fear of death. This is what we see in Jesus who, on his way to the cross, looks over his shoulder to us saying, 'Why should this be the end?' Pain is real, but cannot separate us from the One who is our trusted accompanist. So when the risen Jesus appears to Mary in the garden on the first Easter Day, his word is a word of gentle invitation: 'Mary! Accompany me.'

I tell these stories of resurrection linked to Genesis because my encouragement to all disciples to experience God's story personally requires us to have a twin focus: personal and corporate; past and present; experiment and tradition. Until a few years ago I was fortunate enough to have 20:20 vision, but now I am having to get used to wearing glasses. If you are long-sighted, perhaps you will be the sort of disciple that can easily focus on Jesus the victorious one, powerfully overcoming death. If you are short-sighted, perhaps you will have a clear view of Jesus the neighbour. Both are true, though we can usually focus on only one at a time. Wearing spiritual glasses may help each one of us so that we can see clearly what otherwise might not be in focus. This is the 'invention' of faith. I use the word 'invention' in its original meaning: *to come into being.* We invent the faith both by entering into the tradition and also by adding our own experience to it too. In Vermeer's painting *Woman holding a balance*, your eye is initially drawn to the beautiful woman delicately holding a small balance, ready to weigh out some gold or pearls. She seems calm; the scales are still; it is a moment of pure poise. But if you look behind her, on the wall there is a painting of the Last Judgement. Vermeer has arranged the composition so that the woman is perfectly framed by the frame holding the Last Judgement. Present experience and tradition are in harmony, each heightening the meaning of the other.

So far, I have been reflecting on the third element of the classic evangelical preaching that I heard as a student: personal conversion. Stories and theology can only point others to the door wherein I went. The mild corrective that I want to suggest to this evangelical emphasis is that conversion can be triggered by any aspect of the gospel of Jesus and is not solely to be based on cross and resurrection. I know of disciples who live tremendously authentic dedicated lives, for whom the key story is, say, the parable of the good Samaritan. If challenged, they will acknowledge the theological crux of Good Friday and Easter Day; but for them the spiritual nodal point is this parable. This is what makes the rest of the story of Christ come alive for them.

It has been said that everyone has one good book inside them that could (but may never) be written. I have often changed this slightly to claim that everyone has one good sermon inside them. As a parish priest, it has been my joy and privilege at times to coax such sermons out of people. My task is to create the right contexts so that honest, true and authentic speaking happens. The disciple's task is to resist the voices of embarrassment, awkwardness or lack of self-confidence, and to find the courage to be, in this moment, the mouthpiece of our faith. This involves the re-enchantment of the tradition, not changing what is believed by others, but adding some specific personal details so that others are touched over again by the excitement of God.

In a verse full of encouragement, 1 Peter 3.15 states: 'Always be ready to [give] an account of the hope that is in you.' The first part of this verse requires any disciple to be honest in heart and mind, and draw together the memories, events and thoughts that give shape to their hope. As years pass, the hope may change but it will always be there. Once ready, it is likely the opportunity will arise as people are attracted to authentic hope-bearers. Be ready to give an account, for enquirers will come. As I have said before, inspired disciples are inspiring disciples. Trust that. It's true.

References

Blair, J. (2006), *The Church in Anglo-Saxon Society*. Oxford: Oxford University Press.

Bolt, R. (1996), *A Man for All Seasons*. London: Methuen Drama.

Bradley, F. H. (2001), *Essays in Truth and Reality*. Oxford: Elibron Classics/Clarendon Press.

Dillistone, F. W. (1968), *The Christian Understanding of the Atonement*. Philadelphia, Penn.: Westminster Press.

Foot, S. (2009), *Monastic Life in Anglo-Saxon England, c. 600–900*. Cambridge: Cambridge University Press.

Grayling, A. C. (2011), *The Good Book: A secular bible*. London: Bloomsbury.

Lampedusa, G. T. di (2007), *The Leopard*. London: Vintage Classics.

McClure, J. and Collins, R. (eds) (2008), *Bede's Ecclesiastical History of the English People*. Oxford: World's Classics.

MacCulloch, D. (2009), *A History of Christianity: The first three thousand years*. London: Allen Lane.

MacIntyre, A. (1996), *Whose Justice? Which Rationality?* London: Duckworth.

MacIntyre, A. (2007), *After Virtue: A study in moral theory*. Notre Dame, Ind.: University of Notre Dame Press.

Montefiore, S. S. (2011), *Jerusalem: The biography*. London: Weidenfeld and Nicolson.

Pullman, P. (2010), *The Good Man Jesus and the Scoundrel Christ*. Edinburgh: Canongate.

Thwaite, A. (ed.) (1990), *Philip Larkin: Collected poems*. London: Faber and Faber.